D0242362

How To Talk
Your Way To The Top

How To Talk
Your Way To The Top

EDWARD J. HEGARTY

Parker Publishing Company, Inc.
West Nyack, New York

© 1973 *by*

PARKER PUBLISHING COMPANY, INC.

West Nyack, N.Y.

*All rights reserved. No part of this
book may be reproduced in any form or
by any means, without permission in
writing from the publisher.*

Reward Edition . . . . . October 1978

Library of Congress Cataloging in Publication Data

Hegarty, Edward J
   How to talk your way to the top.

   1. Success. 2. Oral communication. 3. Inter-
personal relations. I. Title.
HF5386.H36   658.4'52   72-13054

Printed in the United States of America

Introduction

TALK YOUR WAY TO THE "TOP" YOU CHOOSE

I say, "Talk your way to the top," and you may ask, "What do you mean TOP?"

The manager's job in my department?
The top job in my company?
The president of my club or lodge?
The councilman from my ward?

Select any top you want to move toward. No matter what it is, I'll state this—The ability to speak so that others understand you can help you get to your TOP.

It can help you more than any other skill you can develop.

And here is the good news—the ability to make what you say clear to others is easy to develop.

You may ask, "If this is such an important skill, and it is easy to learn, why don't more people like me acquire it?"

My thought is that they go about the learning backwards.

They feel they need to learn more words.

They start a vocabulary-building spree that gives them a number of most impressive words—big words, strange words, more precise words.

They forget the main idea of all speech—to help the listener understand.

That's what this book is about—the kind of speech that can be understood by—

members of your family
your supervisors at work
your associates
your employees
the people you meet socially
any individual who can influence your climb to your TOP.

If you speak so these people understand, you can go far. You can—

move up to the better jobs
get the choice assignments from your boss
get elected to the higher offices in your club or lodge
be a leader in your family
become more popular with everybody.

Think of your friends or associates who have this skill. They get the preference, don't they?

Well, don't envy them, join them.

Think of one of the assistants your boss seems to rely on—

his words tell you the kind of person he is, don't they?
you rate him as competent, don't you?
you feel he knows what he is talking about, don't you?

Follow the advice in this book and your listeners will get similar ideas about you. The advice will help you work toward any TOP you select.

Ed Hegarty

CONTENTS

7

make a better impression • Lawyers can approach clarity • Technical words have simple substitutes.

Forget the professor's words • Think of these losses • Employees rate you by their ability to understand you • Too many words don't tell it as it is • Blame it on polarization • Don't try to talk like a manager.

How letter-writers have done it • Your words date you • Your phrases may give the wrong picture • Beware of the old stuffed shirt • Add life to a statement by using more modern language • Check this effort of mine • Let the past stay past • You gain by modernizing.

Part IV

How to Keep Your Big Mouth from Holding You Back

How to check yourself on this fault • Review your day • Check the other's attention • Check what he told you • How we waste words • Take this advice from a sixth grader • How to stop talking too much • Ask others • Limit any group discussion • Listen twice as long as you talk • Talk a bit, then pause • Cut the answers to questions • One point at a time.

Greetings • Same closing • Same designation • The same modifier • The same expression • Cut the familiar "you know." • The same cliché over and over • Five easy steps to better speech habits.

Check how you rate as a "no" man • How do you respond to greetings? • Do you accept news with approval? • How do you talk about the ideas of others? • How do you give advice? • How do others approach you? • How to change to the positive side • Use a positive response to greetings • Cheer the good luck of others • Develop some positive statements • Listen to ideas and ask questions • Offer to help • Ask, "What's my real reason for being negative?" • Say something good • Say "that's good" more often • Who wants "no" men? • Some "no's," yes, but not always.

Listen to the advertisements • Check yourself on this liability • Do others let you talk on? • Do you alibi much? • How do you accept advice or criticism? • How long since you admitted a mistake? • Why positivity is easy to correct • Use questions instead of opinions • Forget alibis • Take advice with thanks • Learn from criticism • Try "I had that trouble." • Assume partial responsibility for employees' mistakes • Say "it was my fault" more often.

Eight ways to show the right attitude • Speak as if you like your work • Associate with the other's problems • Let others work with you, not for you • Never question intelligence • Don't downgrade the jobs or the work of others • Watch status inference • Pay attention to all • Don't fawn on the brass • The right attitude can carry you far.

A time for worriers • What talk of your worries does to you • How to avoid becoming a worrywart • Ask yourself, "What was I worrying about this time last month?" • Reject all worries you can't do something about • Cover yourself with work • Try a bit of optimism.

How complaining holds you back • Your memory • Your work overload • Your feelings • Your health • The cooperation you get from others • The rejection of your ideas • How to stop complaining • Get on the positive side • Check your work procedures • Don't assume personal affronts • When to complain and how to complain • Think of complaints as dust and soot.

wonders if you want him to understand • Your employee makes mistakes • Your employee takes unjustified blame • Others can listen only so fast • Check yourself on speaking speed • Six ways to slow down • Use the pause • Ask a question • Ask what or how • Try repetition • Study your favorite TV voice • Try this slow down exercise • There is no advantage to talking fast • Help him hear and understand.

How poor enunciation handicaps you • The listener doesn't hear • He downrates you • He feels you are trying to impress • How to check your enunciation • Check other speakers • How to correct these faults • The "git" fault • The "yes" fault • The "ing" fault • The "you" fault • Practice with your name • Try reading aloud.

Three ways voices bother others • Your sound • Your attitude • The condition of your health • How to make your voice more pleasant • Consult a voice teacher • Study a book on voice improvement • Analyze your favorite announcer • Read aloud to your wife • Read children's stories to children • Recite poetry • Join in any group singing • Use a recorder • Does your voice help you more?

How To Talk
Your Way To The Top

Part I

HELPING OTHERS STAY TUNED IN ON YOU

You live in a time of too much yak-yak. Think of the voices calling out to you every hour of every day—announcers, newsmen, commentators, advertisers, politicians, educators, and pleaders for causes. Add to that members of your family, your boss at work, your associates, employees, neighbors, friends, and social contacts. TIME magazine called our reaction to the confusion brought to us by this deluge of words "semantic aphasia." The essay said, "Words now seem to cut off and isolate—to cause more misunderstandings than they prevent " A news commentator puts it, "We are drowning in words." A writer said, "It is as if some power had dropped a round transparent cylinder about us so that the words trying to reach us hit the cylinder and bounce away."

Yes, most of us have developed great skill in tuning out. We resort to that semantic aphasia. We pull down that transparent cylinder. Others do likewise; they tune out when we speak. This is why it will pay any individual working toward his selected TOP to study words. Skill with words will help him make his way toward his TOP easier.

1

Getting Yourself a High Intelligence Rating by Helping Others Understand You

If others understand you—

you are rated smarter
others feel you know what you are talking about.

Those two impressions help in any advancement. It pays to help others understand you.

Let's say you sit down at the busy lunch counter at the airport. You want a hamburger fast because others are boarding your flight right now. With the right words you can get that hamburger fast. Without them, the plane may be long gone before your order comes out of the kitchen.

You might ask, "How can anyone get such an order confused?"

It may not be easy, but I saw it done the other day. A stranger moved onto the stool beside me and told the girl, "Get me a hamburger fast."

The girl took the order and some minutes later, when the

hamburger had not arrived, the man asked, "Where's my hamburger?"

"Oh, were you in a hurry?" the girl asked. "I thought you wanted it cooked fast." To her, "fast" meant *well done.*

The man turned to me and asked, "What words could I have used to make it clearer to her?" From his experience he knew that most such misunderstandings are caused by the words the speaker uses.

To make your meaning clear, the listener must—

hear the word you used
know the word you used
give it the same meaning you do.

It does no good to protest, "I know what I mean." The listener must know what you mean. That's what the advice in this book is about—using words that help others understand what you mean.

That ability can help you to success in any activity.

Tell Others What You Mean

If you are to get to your TOP, others must understand you Have you ever asked yourself these questions—

Does my boss understand me?
Do my employees understand me?
Do the PooBahs of my lodge understand me?
Do the people at home understand me?

This should be your first objective in any move toward any TOP—Help others understand you.

Very few people will tell you that they don't understand you. They let you talk on and on. And what is their rating of you if they don't understand?

You're confusing—that s the generous appraisal.

You don't know what you are talking about—they don't, so they assume you don't.

You are a screwball, a crackpot—perhaps dangerous, and they want no more of you.

They surely don't think of you as intelligent, competent, promising.

Your boss doesn't think of you when a promotion is discussed.

The officers of your club don't think of you as officer material.

Your family accepts you as one of the penances the good Lord has inflicted on them.

Learn to help people understand and they rate you higher— You become promotable.

You are noticed by the club officers.

You become a member in good standing with the family.

Words can help do all that for you.

Start Improvement Right Now

I have said that it is easy to improve your ability to help others understand what you say. Here's a way to check me on this. Later in this chapter I give a number of ideas on how to check if others understand you. If the idea is new to you, try it. If it works, I'm sure you will keep on using it. If you know the idea and are not using it, ask yourself why. In a short time, by using such devices, you will see improvement in your skill at helping others understand.

How to Check on the Clarity of What You Say

The listener asks, "What do you mean by that?"

That question tells you that the other hasn't understood, but very few listeners will ask that. They listen and assume they know what you mean, or they don't understand and figure it is your story and so what? Here are some devices that can help you check to see if others understand you:

1. Ask, "Am I Making Myself Clear?"

If you see an expression on the listener's face that indicates he may not understand, ask that question. Most listeners feel it shows weakness if they admit they don't understand. This is true of people who work for you.

2. Ask, "What Are You Going To Do First?"

This question will help if you have made an assignment. If you have a worker who seems to want to get going with the assignment without waiting for full instructions, his answer to this question may tell you that he hasn't understood.

3. Ask the Listener to Tell the Story Back to You

This is a device used by trainers to find out if the listeners have understood. As the story is told back, you discover where you have not made yourself clear.

4. Don't Blame the Listener

You can't excuse yourself by saying—

Those dumb clucks just can't understand
or
They don't listen when I tell them.

Recognize the fact that it is your job to help others understand you.

You have probably heard the character in a TV skit say as he answers the telephone, "Start talking; it's your dime." You laugh at that line, but it describes the spot you are in when you speak to anybody. It's your dime; you're responsible for making the listener understand.

Last week I was in the office of an executive of a large manufacturer when a young man came in to report to him. I offered to leave the office but the executive told me to sit still while the young man talked. "I want your opinion," he said.

I was impressed with the manner in which the young man handled the report he brought in. He spoke well and with as few words as possible. When the young man was gone, I said, "That young man can go far."

The big man agreed, "Yes, he can. Wouldn't it be great if more young men would learn that knack?"

B. C. Forbes said, "Speaking is essential to success in business and the whole of human activities."

That covers everything you do in—
business
social and
fraternal activities.

You'll get along better if you learn to say your piece with clarity.

Remember—it is your dime; protect your investment.
To move up—say your piece clearly; help the listener understand.

You can move steadily toward your TOP as you work to acquire this knack.

2

Using the Right Words to Help Your Listener Hear and Understand

You Can't Use All the Words You Know in Speaking

Who says?
I say it.
And, as the character warns in the TV commercial, "You'd better believe it."

A chart used in my speech clinic using the wording in the first sentence of this chapter always starts an argument. A man tells me, "I can speak any word I know."

He is right at that. He can speak any word he knows. And, if he is talking to himself, there is nothing wrong with his speaking any word he knows.

Writing, Yes; Speaking, No

He can use the word in a letter or a written report. The reader has a chance to look at the word, to study it, and, if necessary, to look up its meaning, but in speaking the listener has only the time

24

needed to hear the word. He doesn't have time to study it. If he pauses to think about the word, he loses some of the meaning of what is being said. Not too many people understand this difference between words that are good for writing and those good for speaking.

Last night the wordy announcer on the football game said, "I don't mean to derogate this player's ability."

The man was speaking to millions. How many of his listeners do you think knew what "derogate" meant? He might have used: discount—knock—criticise—run down—belittle—did you think of depreciate? I am sure that more listeners would know what he meant if he had used any of those words. But he was displaying his large vocabulary and wasn't thinking of those who wouldn't understand.

Six Reasons Why You Can't Speak Every Word You Know

Some of these reasons can be blamed on your listener; others are your fault.

1. The Listener Won't Know the Word

You may say, "I don't use words anybody won't know." That's fine. I believe that most of us feel that our words are simple enough for anyone to understand. But listen to the professionals on TV and you will find them using words like sophistry—loquacious—obfuscation—sporadic—cacophany—meiotic—apopemtic—accretion—taciturn—expatiate. I heard these words not in speeches, but in conversations. Any of those words might be all right for writing, but if you speak such words, not too many of the listeners will know what you mean.

2. The Listener Won't Hear the Word

This happens often as you listen to TV. You did not hear what the man said and you ask your wife, "What did he say?" She replies, "I didn't hear it either." That is togetherness, but if you are the speaker, it doesn't help you one bit. Chapter Nine gives examples of the kind of words your listener won't hear and offers advice on how to avoid them.

Last evening I heard the line, "Hot-heads that go off half-cocked." A listener might have some trouble hearing that. It might be easier to hear if it was, "Hot-heads that make decisions too fast." Too many of the words spoken at us are like blips on the radar screen—they go too fast.

3. The Listener May Give the Word a Different Meaning Than You Do

A commentator on TV says, "unjustified clarity and unjustified obscurity." Again you know the words and could say what you thought he meant, but why waste your time? The golf expert on the TV show says, "Notice how he gets his left side out of the way." Later another says, "Watch how his belt buckle is facing the direction he wants the ball to go." Both are giving almost the same bit of advice. The "left side" may indicate a number of moves, one move to one listener, another move to another listener. But the "belt buckle" picture can leave little doubt.

You may say, "I'm not a commentator or a golf expert." Ok, let's look at some phrases you might use: under active consideration —informed sources—reorient the group—spearhead the issue—give him the picture—give us the benefit of your current thinking. Any of these statements, all in words we know, can be interpreted in a number of ways.

4. The Listener Doesn't Expect the Word

The listener is more likely to understand words he expects. Use an unfamiliar word with him and he may have to pause to try to determine what you mean.

Let's assume you want to say, "You and your group." You have words to substitute for group, such as: aggregation—army—band—bevy—covey—cabal—clan—clique—combine—comrades—constituents—corps—cortege—faction—fraternity—flock—galaxy—gang—guild—herd—horde—menagerie—mob—multitude—party—posse—retinue—squad—syndicate—team—tribe—throng—troups. Yes, you have a great choice of words to apply to those cohorts of his, but by using the familiar, he feels you are referring to his group in a way that carries no special meaning.

5. The Listener Resents the Word

A word that arouses an unfavorable emotion won't help the listener understand. Call his department a "mob" and he feels you are disparaging him and his. After such an unfortunate appraisal he tunes you out. Anything you say makes no sense to him. If your words reflect on such things as the intelligence of his group, its national origin, religion, race, or ability, you close his mind against anything further you say. What you say can classify you as a bigot, racist, or even the patriotic conservative you picture yourself to be.

WORDS THAT SHOCK

These words are poor for speaking for the same reasons. Youngsters are attracted to them; they feel such words are great for throwing over the generation gap. One of the boys in the neighborhood carried our newspaper in his high school days. His customers thought highly of him and made up a purse for him when he went off to college. He has been in college for two years now, and the other day I saw him and talked to him for a while. In our conversation he made these four cracks—

"What would you expect from a racist country?"
"You can only counter force with force."
"The American Revolution was founded on violence, wasn't it?"
"How can a black get a fair trial in this country?"

How did I feel after listening to this type of hogwash? Would I recommend the young man for a job?

Perhaps he was saying these things to shock me. He did that all right, but he went further. He changed my opinion of him completely. The object of any talk is to help the other understand. When you add another purpose you complicate matters. If I were the type to applaud those half-baked statements, the words may have been all right, but he wasn't trying to recruit me. He was trying to show what he thought of me and my generation.

6. You Speak Too Fast

This is perhaps the main fault of most of us. Assume you are the young man who has the job of announcing the hymns to be sung at the church service. Your listeners have to hear three things—the name of the hymn, the number of the hymn in the hymnal, and the number of the page on which it will be found. The young man who had this job at our church spoke all three too fast. I suggested to him that since he would find it difficult to slow down on the name of the hymn, he slow down on the two numbers. He did that, pronounced the two numbers distinctly, and he told me he got a number of compliments from the parishioners. This slowing down is so important that I have devoted all of Chapter 29 to it.

See Why You Can't Speak All the Words You Know

I have given you six main reasons; some are your fault, and others are faults of your listener's hearing. But since your objective is to be understood, it will pay you to speak only words that the listener will hear and understand. Try using all of the words you know in speaking and you might make it a bit more difficult to reach your TOP.

3

You Know Enough Words Now

I do?

Yes, you do.

That statement tells you this is not a book on vocabulary building. It isn't. My claim is that you don't use half of the words you now know. Why learn new words when you don't use many good speaking words you already know?

How Many of These Words Do You Know but Don't Use?

To indicate the man was saying something, you might use: speaking—talking—saying—stating—questioning—babbling—shouting—yelling—and scores of others, for you know all of those words. But you never use some of them, right?

To describe how the man uses words, you might use: fluent—garrulous—glib—gushing—prolix—talkative—verbose—voluble—wordy—effusive—exuberant—you know most of those words. How many do you use?

To illustrate the mood of the speaker, you might use: complaining—grousing—crabbing—beefing—arguing—contending—debating—disputing—quarreling—wrangling. You know those words. Again there are some you never use.

To show another mood: agreeing—accepting—approving—conceding—concurring—praising—complimenting—applauding—commending.

You know every one of those words and its meaning, but how many of them do you use in speaking? This is one of my reasons for saying, "You know enough words now."

The Listener Wants to Understand

You don't need new words to help you. Think of this—when you were a baby, you had no trouble making yourself understood without words. You let out a yelp and the whole family ran to give you service. Then you started to speak, and even in those early days you had little trouble making yourself clear. Next you enrolled at school and learned more words. As you progressed to high school, some of the new words you learned seemed to hide your meaning rather than express it. Listeners started asking, "What did you say?" I heard one teacher describe this problem with, "The words you use seem to get in the way of your meaning. You probably have an associate that fellow workers call "a walking dictionary," but does his store of impressive words make his meaning clearer to you? You want to make your meaning clear to your listeners, and right now you have enough words to do that.

Don't Be Misled by the Vocabulary Builders

The vocabulary builders give you plans for learning new words. One such tells you—

1. See a word
2. Look up its meaning
3. Use it three times in conversation and it is yours.

Steps one and two are good advice. Learn all the words you can. We think with words and we can do a better job of thinking if we have more of the tools, but you can't speak all of the words you learn. Here's an example: Let's assume the new word you learned was—

acronym

You couldn't use that word in conversation because the listener might wonder what you meant. The word means a name made up of the first letters of the words or syllables of other words. Organizations and companies are named with acronyms: ARCO—WESCO—UNESCO. To help the other understand it might be better to say, "It's one of these made-up words like UNESCO that uses the first letters or syllables of a number of words." If the teacher helping you to build a vocabulary gives you this three step rule, follow it. But when you come up with a word like "acronym" rate it a poor speaking word, because not too many listeners will know what it means.

You have heard the vocabulary builder who learns one of these new impressive words and then tries to drag it into every conversation. You figure that the fellow is a show-off, right?

Clarity Pays Off for the Listener and for You

In the newspaper this week a columnist advised young people, "Get your vocabulary out of a rut by substituting more expressive words for words you use often." The words selected as examples were—

soul
nitty gritty
up tight
put on

The suggested substitutions were—

sensitivity for soul
essence for nitty gritty
tense for up tight
misled for put on

32   YOU KNOW ENOUGH WORDS NOW

You may say, "I don't use any of these "youth" words. That's
fine, but note how the substitutions clarify what the speaker means.
The fad words may show you are with it, but the substitutes come
closer to telling the listener what you mean specifically.

How to Add Variety with Clarity

You may want to add variety to your speech, but watch that
in striving for variety you don't sacrifice clarity. Put clarity first.
Let's say you want to say—

"He was speaking to Chuck."
Using words you now know, you could make that—
babbling to Chuck
sounding off to Chuck
screaming to Chuck
complaining to Chuck
beefing to Chuck
bellyaching to Chuck
giving Chuck an earfull

The list demonstrates that you know plenty of words to express
your meaning, and to give variety to your speech, without learning
scores of impressive words that may add to the world's confusion.
You may say, "Some of those substitutions you selected are slang."
That's true, they are—but they express the ideas well, don't they?
At times that slang expression may add feeling and power to what
you say.

CHECK THE CONFUSERS

Think a second—what group of speakers seems to confuse you
most? Isn't it the educated? I find it so, and it seems such a shame.
The college presidents, the PhD's, the professors, the campus radi-
cals, all try to tell it as it is, and the ideas are lost in verbal fog. These
men know more words than you and I will ever know, but their word
knowledge seems to handicap them in making what they say clear
to us. You hear them on TV in panel discussions stirring up fog with
the words and word combinations they use. If you have a youngster

in college you have, no doubt, seen how some of this confusion has been absorbed into his or her vocabulary. One of my friends, when asked what his son is studying in college, replies, "I think he is majoring in mumbo."

How to Build a Vocabulary for Speaking.

In my book, MAKING WHAT YOU SAY PAY OFF (Parker Publishing Co.), I gave these suggestions for building a speaking vocabulary:

1. Survey Your Word Needs

You have certain types of speaking to do in business and in social contacts. Study the type of vocabulary you need to handle these jobs. In most cases you'll find that you know enough words now.

2. Rate the Words You Now Know for Speaking

Of the words you have acquired to date, Chapter Two pointed out that there are some that do not speak too well. Use these in your letters or other writing efforts, but don't try to use them in speaking.

3. Add New Words This Way

When you see a word you don't know in print, write it down. Later, look up its meaning in the dictionary. Now you know the meaning of the word.

4. Rate Any Word You Learn for Speaking

If you didn't know the meaning of the word and had to look it up, it is possible that some of the people who hear you use it might not know the meaning either. Why not rule it out as a speaking word for you?

HERE'S AN EXAMPLE

Assume the word you read was—

perspicuity

You looked up the definition and found it meant clearness in expression, or easy in being understood. You didn't know the word "perspicuity," but you know every word in those two definitions. Then why do you need the word, "perspicuity," as a speaking word?

Don't Depreciate Your Word Knowledge

It has gotten you this far, hasn't it? And it can carry you further. In a discussion session the other day, I asked a man sitting next to me why he didn't speak up. He said, "Because my vocabulary is not on a par with these men who are talking."

"Speak up anyway," I advised, "your opinion is wanted and needed as much as the thoughts of these fellows, who are doing most of the talking."

He started to give his views and what he said made sense.

If you feel that your vocabulary is not adequate when you are in a group, speak up anyway. Perhaps your simpler words will help keep the discussion nearer to earth.

Add All the Words You Desire

Don't allow what I have said to stop any vocabulary-building activity on your part. Learn all the words you can. Remember that what I say is about words for speaking—many of the words you learn will be of no use in speaking. For instance, that word I mentioned—

acronym

What percentage of the people at your job location would know what you mean if you used it?

Then to describe how a man used words, I used—

prolix

Wouldn't a speaker have a better chance of being understood if he had used—

fluent—garrulous—talkative—verbose?
And how about—
windy—wordy—always yakking?

The examples demonstrate how the words you know are often better in helping the listener understand than any impressive new word that you might learn. Word study can be fun, and it can be useful—but don't speak the new words you learn unless you think most of your listeners will understand what you mean.

You Know Enough Words Now

I repeat—the words you know have brought you this far. You don't need a lot of new and impressive words to make it to your TOP. I feel that this is a break for you—instead of looking for new words, practice using the words you know but seldom use.

These Three Ideas Simplify Speech Improvement

The three ideas offered in the chapters ahead can speed your efforts toward more effective speech.

1. Help the listener understand. Make that the purpose of all speaking you do. The one who is understood makes a good impression.
2. Speaking is different from writing in that you can't use all of the words you know. The listener may not know the word, he may not hear it, or he may give it a different meaning than you do.
3. You know enough words now. You don't have to look for a lot of new impressive words to improve your speaking.

Agree with these basics. Try to make everything you say clear to the listener; if possible, use words he might use, and forget trying to impress anybody with your vast vocabulary. Concentrate on faults you may have. The following chapters give you many devices that can help.

Part II

HOW TO MAKE SURE YOUR "ON-THE-JOB" SPEAKING HELPS YOU

You have three kinds of "on-the-job" speaking—at work, in social and fraternal activities, and at home. At work there are friends to make and superiors to impress, and your speech carries most of that load.

It is much the same on the social, civic, or fraternal merry-go-round. Here your listeners have little but your speech by which to judge you.

It is no different at home. Talk to your wife and youngsters with the same deference you use with your boss and you'll get a higher rating, right?

As you read the chapters in this part of the book, study the advice given. Ask yourself, "Am I handling such situations right or wrong?" If you are handling the situation right, fine. If you are not handling it as advised, try changing. It is by trying that you improve. Try one bit of advice today, another tomorrow. Step by step you'll find yourself moving toward your TOP.

4

Talking "Right" to Your Boss

Years ago I read this wisecrack—"Tell your boss what you really think of him and the truth can set you free."

The line is good for a smile, but it speaks truth. Talk one way to your boss and you find yourself out on your ear. Talk another way to him and you find yourself "moving up." It all makes sense.

Your boss is the key man in your advancement to the TOP in your company. How you talk to him can win his confidence, earn his respect, and have him think of you as one of his boys. Here is some advice that can help you build character with your boss.

1. Talk As He Wants It

Every time I tried to explain an idea or plan to one of my bosses he asked, "Got anything on paper about this?" He didn't want to spend time talking in generalities; he wanted something specific to talk about. His question told me how he wanted information brought to him. In putting something on paper, the one who advanced the idea or plan had to do some thinking about it.

This manager wanted some evidence of that thinking. I saw this idea carried a step further when an assistant of mine complained to me that the head of the department in which he worked would not read his proposals.

"How do you give them to him?" I asked.

"I have them typed double spaced."

After some talk we decided the manager didn't want to read four or five pages of typewriting, and so we worked out a plan of giving him a visual presentation. We took a large sheet of paper, about 17 by 22 inches, and drew squares on it. In each square we lettered a headline describing a part of the proposal. When the assistant walked into the office, the big man asked, "What have you got there?"

With the visual presentation displaying the main points, the assistant got all of the time he wanted. After that first reception he visualized every plan he was trying to sell on the same kind of large paper. The big man kidded him about the idea; he called the young fellow, "Big Sheet Chuckie." By giving the manager what he wanted, he got his ideas the attention they deserved. We know that most managers would rather look at a picture than read, so why not give them a picture?

If all your manager wants is an outline, give him that. Most executives want as little talk as possible. If you have doubts as to how your boss wants ideas brought to him, ask, "Is this the way you'd rather have ideas brought to you?" This or a similar question will help you get his idea of how you should talk to him.

2. Talk About His Interests

If his main interest at the moment is cost cutting, try to get that angle into any proposal you make. If his interest is more production or fewer mistakes, talk in these areas will be of benefit.

To help in understanding his interests, you might ask him to outline his main objectives to you. The more you know about him, his thoughts and feelings about his work, the more you can help him. One friend who went to work for a new boss told me, "I have always been against coffee breaks, but my new boss is for them. He likes to sit down with the girls and talk over a cup of coffee." The friend added, "I've got a lot of arguments against coffee breaks, but I won't use them on this job."

Take a piece of paper and write on it a list of your supervisor's main interests—

Cost cutting
More production
Absenteeism
Politics
Golf
Pittsburgh Pirates

Note that some of the subjects suggested have little to do with the job, but if your boss is a Pirate fan, it can't hurt if you know the names of the Pirate players and check the box scores each day. When he speaks of his heroes you can seem a dummy to him if you don't know what he is talking about.

One of my neighbors came up to my yard the other day and asked me, "Ed, I have a boss who's nuts about cost cutting. He turns down my ideas with, 'We're trying to cut costs, not add to them.' How can I lick that?"

One example he gave was that he wanted to move a row of accounting machines. When he proposed it, the boss thought of the cost of moving the machines, not of the efficiency that would be gained by the move. My advice was, "Start your story with the cost-saving benefit." For instance, "We can operate these machines with three men instead of four if we move them." The saving of one man means a cut in payroll, the largest expense in any operation. The man tried that plan, and he came back to thank me for the idea. "He listens to my ideas when I use that approach," he said.

I have suggested to junior executives that when they see an article in a newspaper or trade paper on a subject of interest to their boss, they clip the article and send it to him. One man who did this said, "He called me into his office to discuss the article. Good thing I read it, isn't it?" His question indicates that he thought of this as a trick. This type of thing is not a trick. It can be most important in helping an aspirant to get to his TOP. Find the boss' interests and talk about them.

3. Offer To Help

On any job there are certain tasks that nobody likes to do. One company I know had a forecasting policy that called for five and ten year guesses. This company had its supervisors working with figures two to three days each month. None of the men liked the work. They didn't believe in the forecasts arrived at; they didn't feel that anybody above paid any attention to them. Then a smart assistant asked if he couldn't work out a fast slide-rule way to make the forecasts without everybody spending two days juggling figures. The boss agreed, and the assistant came up with a plan. Management got its figures, but the supervisors saved the time to work at their jobs.

Your immediate supervisor may have tasks that he might delegate to you if he knew you were willing. If your supervisor is covered with work, ask him,

"Is there any way I can help?"

This type of request shows you are willing to work. You know that one of management's complaints is, "Nobody wants to work any more." Desire to work and you will attract attention. One man who tried this at my suggestion told me, "That's lousy advice; you know what he gives me—only stinkers." But by taking those tough jobs he was helping, wasn't he?

CHECK YOUR PERFORMANCE BEFORE OFFERING TO HELP

Before offering to help, make sure that you are doing a good job on the tasks assigned to you. If you are handling your assigned tasks sloppily, don't ask for more interesting work—you might get a bawling out. Check how the boss feels you are doing on your current assignments first.

Use these reasons when you offer help—

I want to learn more about the work of the department.

I would be interested in something more challenging.

Make sure that your own job is being handled well before you offer to help. Don't stick your neck out if you are vulnerable.

4. Bring Problems, but Suggest Solutions

Most supervisors have problems of their own. When an assistant brings another problem, they would like him to suggest a solution. One manager showed me a card he had framed on his office wall. It read, "DON'T BRING ME A PROBLEM WITHOUT YOUR SUGGESTION FOR A SOLUTION." As he showed me the sign, he said, "I show that to every new man who joins the department. It saves a lot of time I might spend in talking."

Don't ask your boss to decide everything unless he insists. One executive told me, "I go you one better on this idea of problems with solutions. I say to the boss, 'I have a problem here and I also have three ways we can move on it.' That's good selling, isn't it—giving him a choice."

Try that idea; work up a question similar to—

"I've got a problem here, and three suggestions for its solution.

Select the one you think best, and I'll start action immediately."

5. Keep Him Informed

Keep the boss informed. He may not be interested in small talk, gossip, or tattle-type yak-yak about other employees, but he is surely interested in any information that affects his department. Many times your grapevine is superior to his. He gets his information through the proper channels; perhaps you get yours through all levels of management, and from those who might not be called management. You know how rumors can spread in a department or company. If you hear a rumor from one of your people, check it out with your boss at once. Let him check it with his higher-ups. Find out what type of information your supervisor wants, then bring that kind to him.

6. Check Your Standing

Many times when I ask men how they are doing on their jobs they tell me, "I guess I am doing all right; nobody says anything." Don't guess how you are doing. Ask your boss. He may give you some tips on things he doesn't like about your work and some suggestions for improvement. He may say, "You are doing fine, just keep it up." Some bosses are like that. That doesn't tell you much, does it? Keep asking. You may get some criticism that is hard to take, but you will let the boss know that you want to do things his way. Ask such questions as—

How am I doing?
Did I handle that Ajax job as you would have handled it?

7. Let Him Help Decide on Training You Might Need

If you are thinking of taking a course in public speaking or rapid reading, ask your boss about it. He may suggest other training that will be of more use to you. If he has a hand in your training, even though it is only through advice, he is likely to take credit for helping you along. Keep him informed about your progress in any course you are taking. His superiors rate him on his ability to train, and your talk about your progress gives him material that he can use with them. Don't be afraid to ask—

"What training do you think I need most?"

8. Shun "Phony" Flattery

You have employees in the office who seem to make a play for the top man with applause, praise, compliments, flattery, and other such acclaim. You may call them "yes" men, cheerleaders, bootlickers, or any of the other names used to describe those who stoop to such tactics. You don't look up to them as heroes, do you? One executive told me, "My boss wants that kind of servility, and I'm not good at it." My advice to him was, "Don't get good at it. It tends to degrade you."

Even when your praise and adulation pleases your boss, psychologists say that he is fooling himself by accepting it—and when he realizes that he is being fooled, who does he blame? Not himself, but his cheering section. How can your boss think of you as anything but a flunky if you are continually buttering him up? How can he believe what you say about any other angle of the business?

Analyze Your Performance

Check through these bits of advice and ask yourself, "How do I rate on each of these?" If you feel you do not rate as high as you should on any of them, start right now doing what's necessary to improve your stand.

I once heard this bit of dialogue between a supervisor and an assistant that he admired. The supervisor made a remark, and the following dialogue ensued:

"Hallelujah, you're a bum," said the assistant.

"You can't call me a bum," said the boss.

"I can if I use the Hallelujah."

"Why does the Hallelujah change it?"

"The Hallelujah means you're also the King."

"That's right," said the supervisor, "Let us not forget that."

The last is good advice. Don't forget who is the King.

If the King likes the way you talk to him, the way you present ideas and plans to him—

you are on your way to your TOP.

5

Talking "Right" to Others About Your Boss

Want to know how to talk about your boss? Take a tip from the members of the President's official family.

When any criticism of the President or his policies is heard in the land, what do they do?

They rush to defend.

There is no doubt who they are for or which side they are on. They are for him—100 percent.

Make that your policy. Let what you say show you are for your boss.

He will like it, and those who hear you speak well of your supervisor will admire your loyalty.

Read that line again.

Those who hear you speak well of your supervisor will admire your loyalty.

Those listeners may hate the innards of your boss.

They may think him a dirty SOB.

But you come off with a good rating from all who hear you because you are loyal. Loyalty inspires admiration. The sly inuendo

or the outright criticism tells the listener that you can't be trusted.
Here is some advice on how to talk about your boss—

1. Show you are for Your Boss.
2. Fight his battles.
3. Protect his status.
4. Boost him and his work.

1. Show You Are For Your Boss

A few years ago I was making a survey of the Chicago market
on the distribution of home laundry equipment. The plan was to call
on every retailer with the salesman who handled the account. One
salesman picked me up early one morning, and before we had gone
two blocks he said, "I don't know who you are, Mister, and you may
be able to get me fired from this job, but this sales manager we've
got is absolutely the dumbest so and so I have ever met."

As we travelled throughout the day, there was more and more
of this. He couldn't see why the top management couldn't see
through the phony. Here was a case where the speaker's big mouth
told me more about the speaker than about the boss. For instance—

He was a complainer.
He perhaps wouldn't like any boss.
He led me to suspect that the quality of his work was undermined
by his attitude.
He didn't seem to be on the company's side.

Add to this list. You probably could think of other things that
such talk would show you.

On that same survey I rode with eight other salesmen who
reported to this same boss. Not one offered a word against him. To
check on how general this feeling about the boss was in each case,
I asked what they thought of their boss—and I never heard a single
complaint. Now who looked bad? These men may have had complaints, but if they did, they never mentioned them.

Maybe in your business you have some fellow workers who
complain about their bosses. If you know such men, ask yourself,
"What chances do they have of getting promoted?"

Tell your boss you are for him.

You don't need to tell him, "Boss, I am on your side."

Use the word "we" when you refer to the company; use "we" when you refer to the department.

Use the word "team" when you speak of a bit of work the department has done. Use such questions as, "Makes you proud of our team, doesn't it?"

Use the word he uses to describe his department. If he uses the word "gang," use the word "gang." The use of the same word he uses shows you agree with him.

2. Fight His Battles

You may ask, "What do you mean, battles? He doesn't have any. He's a Casper Milquetoast type of guy; he wouldn't fight anybody."

If that's the case, maybe he needs your strong right arm even more. Perhaps you wouldn't call his differences battles, but he has a number of managers competing with him for the jobs ahead. Some may fight like gentlemen, but others have their knives out, looking for any advantage they can get.

Let's say another supervisor at the management level of your boss asks, "How can you stand working for that slave driver?"

He says it as if in jest, but you have to remember that one day you might be working for this individual who is trying to sabotage your boss. That's where finesse helps. You might be tempted to say—

"I'd much rather work for him than for you."

That may be 100 percent true, but you don't want to make this supervisor angry. At the same time, you don't want to be disloyal to your boss. What would you say? How about—

"He works harder than he asks any of us to work."
"He's the fairest boss I've ever worked for."
"He rides us for mistakes, but he pats us on the back when we do a good job."

If you answer any saboteur with comments like those, the competitor will look for someone else to pump for information.

Don't be embarrassed by such questions. The questioner is on the attack; come back on the offensive. He won't resent your action. He'd want one of his assistants to rush to his defense, wouldn't he?

3. Protect His Status

A vice-president of a company I worked for gave me quite a hard time once because I hadn't invited his assistant to a dinner for some visiting distributors. "You had all the other men of his rank there and he tells me he wasn't invited. I know you don't like this fellow, Ed, but when you invite others of his rank, you should invite him."

I hadn't handled the invitations; my assistants had, and I don't know why this man was not invited. Perhaps the assistants didn't like him either. But he wasn't invited, and the vice-president was miffed about it.

The man's status may be important to him or it may not. Even when the man disclaims any desire for the trappings of importance, a slight may hurt his feelings. Your immediate boss has a certain status in your company. Perhaps he is conscious of it and fights to protect it.

I had one assistant who opened the door of my office one day and said, "Here's your rug, Mr. Hegarty." I hadn't ordered a rug, but I had been around long enough to know that this was no time to ask questions. The assistant and the two workmen moved the furniture and spread the rug.

When the desk was back in place, I asked the assistant, "What's the story on the rug?"

He said, "I saw they were putting them in offices on the other side, and I told the office manager that you outranked those guys who were getting rugs, and so you got one."

I don't think that the rug on the floor improved my work one bit, but it was a status symbol that the assistant thought I should have.

What should a boss think of an assistant who went out of his way to do a thing like that? He could be mighty sure that the employee wasn't trying to sabotage him, right?

4. Boost Him, His Work, and the Work of His Department

Nobody will tell you that it pays to be a press agent or public relations man for your boss, but I can state this idea with certainty—the individual who speaks well of his boss is building character for himself. Every boss has some good qualities. The list below tells you what men in my Management Clinic say is good about their bosses.

How to Boost Your Boss While You Profit

Mention one of these good qualities. For instance—

1. He's fair.
2. He keeps his cool under stress—no shouting and swearing.
3. He's always cheerful.
4. He makes you feel important.
5. He has a real interest in you as an individual.
6. He backs you up.
7. He pats you on the back now and then.
8. He admits mistakes.
9. He defends his men.
10. He helps you correct your mistakes.
11. He is open to new ideas, new ways of doing things.
12. He gives you a job and lets you do it your way.
13. He shares any blame for mistakes.
14. He is honest with you, tells the truth.
15. He shares credit.
16. He keeps you informed.
17. He's a good teacher—you're learning a lot from him.
18. He gives you a chance to tell your side of the story.
19. He asks you for advice and suggestions.
20. He listens to you.
21. He doesn't look over your shoulder while you work.
22. He doesn't critize in public.
23. He forgets past mistakes.
24. He can do any job in his department.
25. He works harder than you do.

When I congratulated one young man on getting a promotion, he asked, "Know why I got it?"

I told him I didn't.

"The boss says I'm his best public relations man."

The young man had spoken well of his boss at every opportunity, and the boosting had paid off.

There's Plenty of Good to Emphasize

Out of that list, can't you pick some good things to say about your boss? Check back through the list and select the ones that apply. Then, when a critic makes a crack, contribute your "plus" idea. When another supervisor tells how your boss helped him out of a jam, add

"He's like that, and—"

Such talk shows which side you are on.

Show You Are Loyal

Let everything you say show you are—

for your boss
for the management.

It is your department, your company, your opportunity. Boost your boss.

When he moves up, there may be a better job for you. A reputation for loyalty is a great boost in helping you move toward your TOP.

6

Talking "Right" To and About Everybody
Brings Real Popularity

Does everybody around your job like you?

You may say, "I don't care whether these dopes like me or not. My work is what counts."

Forget the attitude shown by those words. Shape up. Your work is important, of course—the quantity, the quality, and other factors—but think of this: one of the first questions asked about a candidate for promotion is—

"How does he get along with other workers?"

How do you get along with others at your job?

In my town, the manager of a large hardware store passed away. About one week later I was in the store and asked an employee friend, "Who will be your new manager?"

"It has to be Jim," he said.

"Why Jim?"

"He's the only one everybody would work for."

"Why would everybody work for Jim?"

"He's one of us; he understands our problems. We feel he would be fair to all of us."

How to Develop a "Get-Along" Personality that Helps You Climb

Here is some advice on how to make more friends—

1. Take Part

Match for the cokes, take a card in the football pool, go to the parties. Join the teams. If the boys want you to try out for the bowling team, even though you protest that you can't bowl, go out for a few sessions and the others will see that you are not the bowler they want. Start activities yourself. I had an assistant who was always running some kind of sport pool, improvement course, trips to ball games, or other such activity. He seemed to know the names and nicknames of every employee in the office and factory. My boss once advised me, "We ought to figure out some way to harness that guy's energy to some job that will benefit the company." I said that what he was doing was helping on morale. The boss agreed to that; the man's taking part got him notice. Take part; it helps you move toward the TOP.

2. Talk Equality

Treat the others in your department as a "one-for-all, all-for-one" operation. When you talk about the work, use such words as—

we can do it—this is our idea, our job, our concern—nobody can beat us

our team—our gang—score another for our team—give the credit to our gang

one of us—our kind—

Chuck is one of us; you'd expect him to do a good job.

We've got the knack of working together.

Every employee wants to belong. You make friends by showing in your talk that you consider this desire in others. Let the workers around you feel that your department is one unit, one family.

3. Show You Think the Other Is Important

Everybody on the payroll thinks he is important. Show by your talk that you think each one is. One manager told me, "When I put a new man on a job, I give him an indoctrination on the importance of what he is doing. If a guy is checking bills from suppliers against receiving slips, he may think his job is one that any clerk can handle. If you show him how much the guy ahead of him on that job saved the company in a few months' time, he feels better about the work."

4. Talk About His Accomplishments

A foreman in a steel mill once told me, "Every man wants to produce." He wants to do his best, he wants his efforts to be appreciated. Recognize this and talk about the good job he does. Let him know that you understand his special skills. When he does well, compliment him, but direct your kind words at some job he has done. Think of such statements as—

"How did you ever come to think of that?"
"That's a clever idea, Bill."
"You're good at handling those people."
"You did those stencils beautifully."

Don't go overboard by praising everything, but a few kind words now and then can help. Also, don't indicate that the element of luck is involved in any job success. The other man says, "I was lucky to catch the mistake." OK, maybe he was lucky, but add, "You were alert, too."

5. Carry Your Share

Don't let anyone call you a Gold Brick. You'll be more popular if you are known as a worker. When employee or club projects are proposed, ask such questions as—

"Got a job for me?"
"What do you want me to do?"
"How about dealing me a hand?"

When you are given a job, get it finished as fast as you can. Show you mean what you say.

6. Show Interest

If an associate is taking a self-improvement course, show an interest. Ask how he is doing, what he likes most about it, what he finds most difficult. Don't offer advice unless he asks for it. Determine exactly what advice he wants before you sound off.

7. Get Personal

If one of the associates has sickness in the family or other troubles, offer to do what you can to help. Make a list of the favors you might do—loan your car, take his kids to school—whatever you can think of that might help. In most cases you won't be able to do anything, but if you find you can do something, move in. If the associate gives you some private information, keep it to yourself.

8. Learn Names and Remember Them

Don't say, "I'm not good at remembering names." Get good at it. The other's name is his most prized possession. You'll get better service anywhere if you know the man's name is Pete, and you call him by name. Then, too, he will think better of you because you used his name. Use first names with older associates only when they ask you to. Until they ask, use Mister. Show you were brought up right.

9. Talk Up the Group's Accomplishments

Speak enthusiastically about the work your group does. This is your job, your department, your activity; boost every phase of it. Boost the company, the management, the objectives, the quality of the work, the good the product does for customers. Find the good things to say and emphasize them.

10. Boost Individuals in Your Group

Maybe they are not the greatest, but on many points they are great. Speak of those great points. Make others feel wanted, needed, important. Each individual is great; the group is the greatest. Follow the plan given in the preceeding chapter on talking about your associates.

11. In Conversation, Play Down Your Interests

If another is interested in baseball and you in football, 'alk baseball. You may think he goes overboard in his admiration f the Cincinnati Reds, but he doesn't think he does. If he is a gardener, ask him questions about his hobby. If he is painting his house, ask about the kind of paint, the brushes, rollers, or what not, and then listen to his ideas.

12. Spread Beyond Any Small Clique

The foursome that plays golf with you every weekend or your "share-the-ride" group are your friends. The other workers know that and accept it. Try to spread your attention outside of these groups. Don't let anybody say, "He's got those three guys he plays golf with and he has no time for anybody else." Have time for everyone.

Practice on the Folks at Home

Bring every one of these devices home with you. The people at home, your wife, your kids and the pets are for you. You are the "greatest" with them. Prove you are the greatest. Forget the wise-cracks about the wife's relatives, the teenagers' long hair, the daughter's monopoly of the telephone. Ask about the youngster's projects. Listen to them as they tell you their stories. Be courteous; use "please" and "thank you." Ask for advice and suggestions.

You may feel your home is your castle, and you are the king. Why not be a good and gracious king? Give the greatest respect to those who live at your house, and you will make life easier for yourself and the ones who are your most sincere friends.

"The Good Guy Always Loses" Isn't True

Most of the suggestions in this chapter add up to being a friend to one and all, a good guy. Be a good guy. As one of my friends puts it, "There is no sense in making anybody sore at you." There isn't. Have as many people as possible think of you as a good guy, and there will be approval as you move up toward your TOP.

It is easy to build a cheering section. Try any one of these devices and see for yourself. In a short time you can get to be an expert at any one of them. As one of my associates says, "It's easier to be a good guy than a meanie."

7

Taking These Same Steps to the Top in Social Groups

Moving up in a club is like moving up in business. Treat the officers as you would your boss, the members as you would your associates on the job. Be a good guy to one and all.

Follow this plan and you can move up in any group.

Leadership Is Needed

Business is looking for leaders. Organizations are looking for leaders.

A club president told me, "Old men are running this club, and we don't have any young men coming up."

Thousands of clubs are in that situation. Think of your club— isn't there room for new leaders?

How To Move Toward Leadership In Any Group

If you want to be a leader in your service club, lodge, fraternity, or trade association, here is some advice on handling yourself:

57

1. Boost the Objectives

If the club has a favorite charity, speak well of that charity. If it works with youth, take part in that work, show you believe in it, enlist other members to work in it. Talk to the man who heads up the activity. Ask how you can help. Talk to other members about it. Explain it to your friends.

Such activities help build your enthusiasm. They show others that you really believe. Members like a man with such an attitude.

2. It Pays to Help the Officers Look Good

One club I belonged to a few years ago elected a short man to be president. When he took over the gavel he was about completely hidden by the giant lectern the club used. The secretary had a small lectern made and he used it at the next meeting. Now the president was not overshadowed by a lectern. The secretary explained the expense to me by saying, "The president is important, right? How can anybody feel important while he is trying to chin himself on a lectern twice as large as he is? A leader should be on top of a soap box, not hiding behind it." That secretary was showing that he was for that president.

Status is as important to some officers of groups as it is to some business executives. The other evening, at a Chamber of Commerce dinner, a friend and I had agreed to sit together at one of the tables in the audience. After we had been seated, one of the officers came and asked the friend to sit at the head table. He argued a bit, but then agreed to move up. He said, "I hate to leave you, Ed." But he didn't hate it; he loved that bit of recognition.

Let the officers of your group know you are for them. Any witticism about the way they handle things makes you look bad. Any criticism may ruin your chances to move up.

Find Out What the Group Needs, and Talk About That Need

Most clubs need more members; some need better programming. Your group has some such need. Find out what it is and do some thinking on it. If the need is for new members, talk to the chairman of the membership committee about the problem; if it is programs, contact the program chairman. Whatever the problem, there is somebody worrying about it. You can be sure that if this individual sees a young man who looks promising, he will be asking, "How can I use this guy and his ideas?"

One young man told me how he had gone to his membership chairman with a suggestion that each member be asked to submit three names of friends who might join his club. The suggestion was taken, the plan put into action, and in a short time the membership was filled to the point where the club had a waiting list for the first time in its history.

Find out the group's problems and talk to those responsible for correcting them. Talk to members of other clubs to see what they did when they had similar problems, then discuss the methods you uncovered with your higher-ups.
Ask—

"How can I help?"
"Give me something to do."

4. Work On Any Assignment

If you are given four cards with the names of prospective members to call on, make the calls and get the cards with answers back to the chairman. Some of the members will mail the cards to the prospects with a note, others will telephone the prospects, and still others will do nothing. The membership chairman can't make a report because so many cards are unreported. When you handle the task promptly, you attract notice. If you ask for more names to call on, you stand out. Get a reputation as a worker and you will be asked to take on more assignments, but that is how you move up—assignment by assignment. All committee chairmen like to hear, "Is there anything I can do?"

5. Show Respect

The officers take their roles seriously. They may feel that you owe respect to the office, if not to the officer. Maybe some of your group call the president, "Old Ironpants." Forget such levity. Perhaps his way of handling the ritual seems amusing to you, but to him the ritual is a serious matter, and he feels his way is best.

Speak with respect of the efforts of all the officers. One of my associates says, "They pick the officers from the cheering section. That's why I have no chance." To move up in a club you need friends. Suppose you tell Joe, "Don makes a good chairman." Joe may think just the opposite, but your positive statement may cause him to ask, "Why does he think Don is good?" Maybe, if you had said, "Don couldn't chairman anything," Joe would agree, and perhaps give you some specifics on why you were so right. But when you said Don was good, you showed your loyalty—and the loyal ones get moved up.

6. Talk Right On Youth vs. Age

You see this in just about every club, lodge, or fraternal organization. The old men run things, and the young bucks want to take over. When you run into such a rhubarb, consider the groups and how they feel about themselves. The oldsters feel that they have made the group what it is today; they have years of experience. The young people feel that they have ideas, and the energy to make those ideas work.

A neighbor, who belonged to a club in which there was this kind of fight, asked me how he could stay neutral. After talking about it, we decided that he might make a comparison of the good of the two groups to the club. He drew a line through the center of a small card. On one side he listed the advantage of age; on the other, the advantage of youth. Then, when he was asked to state his preference, he used his card to outline his views. He told me, "Both sides thought I was being fair, trying to decide which would be best for the club." Later, when he was nominated for an office in the club, he got votes from both sides.

Nick Skorich, when he was made the new coach of the Cleveland Browns football team, was asked if he was going to build with youth or age. He said, "It should be a blend. You need a foundation of experience, with youth coming up." The oldsters go for that "foundation," the youngsters for the implied opportunity. Nick's opinion is one most listeners would agree with. Follow that example when you run into any "youth vs. age" discussion. It helps make friends.

YOU NEED TALK PLUS

You may make a fine impression when you speak out in the meetings, but that impression will not help much if you won't sell the tickets, bring in the membership prospects, or do the other tasks assigned to you. But if you make an impression with your speaking and emphasize it with the work you do, you will go as far as you want to go. I have said that your group is looking for new leaders, the ones who will take over in the future. Train yourself to be one of them. Here it is in a nutshell—

talk loyal
make as many friends as you can, both
officers and members
be willing to work.
Loyalty—friendship—work

Can you think of any stronger recommendations for promotion to your TOP?

If you have any chance of moving up in your club, you are doing many of these things now. Do more of them. Do each job with enthusiasm. Watch the men you think are the coming leaders. They rate well on all of these ideas, don't they. Given some time, you can rate as well as any of them.

Congratulations on Your Progress

You move ahead by using ideas, not by reading about them. You hear about an idea, you try it. If it works, you keep on using it. If it doesn't work, you reject it. In the four chapters in Part Two of this book, you have read of many ways your words can help you score better—on your job, at the club or lodge, and in social gatherings. Not a single one of the ideas is difficult to try, yet how many have you tried? This is how you improve by using what you know. Let's do a bit of checking—

1. Are you talking better to your boss?
2. Have you improved what you say about him?
3. Have you changed your talk to associates and employees?
4. How many of the suggestions on becoming a leader have you tried out?

Don't wait for the bigger ideas that you might find later in the book. The ideas you have already found have helped others improve. You'll find they will do the same for you.

Part III

MAKING SURE WHAT YOU SAY IS CLEARLY UNDERSTOOD

I have said that your listener must—

hear the word you use
know the meaning of the word, and
give it the same meaning you do.

Clarity to your listener is the most important factor in any speaking you do. He has to understand your statements, explanations, orders and assignments. If you wrote him a memo, he could study the written words. He doesn't have that chance with spoken words—they're gone, and he may not remember too well.

The chapters in this part of the book offer you advice on the kind of words to use to help your listener understand.

8

Can You Sound Sincere Speaking Some of the Words You Write?

You have two vocabularies that you use with others—one you use in speaking, you use a different one in writing. If you try to speak some of the words in that writing vocabulary, you sound unnatural.

To check this, try reading aloud the words you might write in a letter. "Yours of the fourth inst" doesn't speak too well. You say, "I wouldn't write it that way in a letter." Good for you. But you get the point.

Tonight on the news program on TV you'll hear men make statements that they or some public relations man wrote. Listen and you'll agree that the man would never use such words if he was explaining his ideas in conversation with you. The words from his writing vocabulary don't speak well. If you know him, you say, "That doesn't sound like Pete." Because the words didn't sound like Pete, you have some doubts about the truth of what he said.

Speak Only Words You Speak Well

The words you speak best are those you use every day with the folks at home and the workers at the job. Forget the other words you know. For instance, you might say—

"remove the rascal"
                or
"throw the bum out"

You know the meaning of all of the words in those orders, but which would sound like you? Use "Remove the rascal" with those who know you and you might get a laugh. Use it with strangers and they'd wonder what manner of man is this.

Check Any Statement You Prepare

Words from your written vocabulary are more likely to work themselves into statements or explanations you prepare for your boss, committees, or other small groups. You will be asked to do many of these on your way to your TOP. To get these bits as short as possible and to allow you to study them, you will want to write them out. This writing helps, but go one step further: try to write only words from your speaking vocabulary. Even if you have to read the piece, the words you normally use in speaking will read better. The listeners will feel that you are speaking, not reading an essay.

How to Use Only Speaking Words for Speaking Prepared Pieces

To get what you say in a meeting or a conference into speaking words, use these devices:

1. Speak from notes
2. Dictate what you plan to say
3. Edit words you seldom speak.

Here are some thoughts on how to do this.

1. Speak From Notes

There is safety in speaking from notes. I advise making some notes on a card any time you go to your boss with an idea. You'll do a better-organized job of explaining, and he will see that you have given some thought to your idea. Make these notes short—just enough words to remind you of the point you want to make. When

you work from notes in speaking to a committee or a group, the
listeners feel

you know what you are talking about
you mean what you say
you believe in the idea.

2. Try Dictating

One way to get away from the use of written words is to dictate.
In dictating you are more inclined to use your speaking vocabulary.
Pick up the mike of the machine and talk fast. If you use contractions
like "don't" and "can't," don't change them to "do not" and "cannot." Ask the girl to type it just as you dictate. Don't stop to think
of the precise word to express the thought. The thinking will dig into
your writing vocabulary. Keep on going.

TALK TO "JOE"

I use a device in dictating to keep me with speaking words. I
dictate to an imaginary Joe, using his name over and over again, like
this: "This is how it is, Joe." "Here is the reason for that, Joe." After
the reason is stated, I ask, "What do you think of that, Joe?" When
I go over the typed piece and cut out all of the "Joes," I find the
device gives me a naturalness that sounds like me. It helps cut the
big words and modifiers that might make me sound like a show-
off.

3. Edit Words You Seldom Speak

In even a few sentences of writing you use words you seldom
speak. Change these to speaking words. Look at every word with
seven or more letters. Examine the vague words, the words with
many meanings. We use more of these in writing than in speaking.

Cut most adjectives because they fight with the nouns. Get the
piece in the type of words you would use with the gang at lunch,
and your listeners will applaud your ability to make yourself clear.

How to Determine if a Word Is One of Your Speaking Words

There follows a list of words. Each line lists a number of words with about the same meaning. Check through the list and decide which of these words belong in your speaking vocabulary, which in your writing vocabulary:

concur—accede—agree—assent—acquiesce
vilify—abuse—knock—blame—curse—defame—denounce
emend—correct—revise—repair—fix—mend—rectify
apathetic—lifeless—numb—sleepy—uninterested—dead
odor—aroma—smell—fragrance—scent—perfume—stink
agitate—confuse—disorganize—muddle—snarl—make trouble
sensitive—touchy—emotional—high-strung—ticklish

In a letter you might use any one of those words, but in a speaking assignment, forget your writing vocabulary. Speak only words that you would use in conversation and what you say will sound as though you are presenting your own ideas—ideas you believe in.

You Benefit by Sounding As If You Believe

I was substituting for my supervisor before a management committee because he had to be out of town. "They'll ask you about how we handle this problem, and here's what I want you to tell them." He had written out a statement for me to make. I read the statement and said, "Let me work this over and check back with you."

"I want you to say exactly what I have there," he protested.

"Let me read it for you." I read the statement as well as I could.

He listened and shook his head. "You don't put any feeling into it. You sound as if you don't believe in the practice."

"I didn't think I could sound sincere. These are your words, your way of saying things. Here, you read it."

He read the statement and it sounded fine. Later, when I revised his statement into my words, he approved with, "I thought we spoke the same language."

"We do, but we don't use the same words."

He could put meaning into his speaking words; I could put meaning into mine. Had I used the statement in his words, I am sure that the listeners would have gotten the impression that I was covering up.

Why Exact Meanings Are Not So Important in Speaking

As the listener listens, he doesn't have time to think, "What exactly does he mean?" Books on writing advise you to search out words with precise meanings, but the exact meaning is not so important in the words you speak. A man says,

"I'm discouraged," or,
"I'm sad about this."

You know there is some difference in the meaning of the words, but if he uses either statement you get about the same idea. The precise word helps in writing (because the reader has an opportunity to study it), but in speaking the exact meaning is not nearly so important.

Your Speaking Words Tell the Listener More

Give your speech in your speaking words and you can show—

more sincerity
more conviction
more enthusiasm
more interest.

The listener is inclined to believe what you say, agree with your idea, do what you ask. His attitude toward you helps you move toward your TOP.

9

Helping Your Listener Hear

If the listener doesn't hear, you have said nothing. Suppose you say—

"The small boy was wary when I asked the questions."

The word "wary" is an example of a word that does not speak well. It is not an unknown word, or one that is complicated, but the listener might ask, "What did you say the boy was?"

The thought that a listener might not understand us because we used a simple word that he did not hear is new to most of us. Check the word you used next time one of the family asks you, "What did you say?" You may say, "He wasn't listening." Maybe not, and then maybe he was, but he didn't hear the word you used.

Now let's think about that word—"wary." There are a number of words you could have used to express the same idea—words that are easier to hear:

cautious
careful
suspicious

These are better speaking words because they give the listener more time to hear what was said. Here are some thoughts on words that are difficult to hear—

1. The One-Syllable Word

What makes the short word difficult to hear?

First, it goes fast, and
Second, we don't take the trouble to pronounce it carefully.

I rate these words poor for speaking—

apt
heed
waive

Try saying each aloud.
You probably took more time than you ordinarily would in saying them and felt you did well, but if you don't take that care, the listener might not hear what you said.

WORDS WITH MORE SYLLABLES SPEAK BETTER

There are three words you might use instead of the ones you just said. Try saying these aloud—

"likely" for "apt"
"listen to" for "heed"
"relinquish" for "waive"

The substitutes mean about the same, and the extra syllables give the listener a bit more time to hear what you said. If you speak rather fast, use more multi-syllable words, not to impress with your word knowledge, but to help your listener hear. Many big words are easily understood.

2. Forget the Unusual or Unexpected Words

The lecturer on the TV said—

"This bodes ill."

I needed a few extra seconds to figure out what he had said. The man said—

"I can't cope with it."

His wife asked, "What is it you can't do with it?"
The commentator said—

"He looked wan."

He might have used these words that are easier to hear—

pale
pallid
tired
exhausted

The announcers at the football game in Denver kept repeating the name of the stadium. Each time they said it, I tried to figure out what they were calling it. Then it dawned on me—

"Mile-High Stadium"

Not because I heard what was said, but because I remembered that Denver called itself the mile-high city.
At another game the announcer said, "In the waning moments of the game." Try improving on that word—

"waning"

Did you come up with:

final—last—closing?

I'm sure your word would be easier to hear than "waning."

SUBSTITUTE EXPECTED WORDS IN THESE SENTENCES

"I can't 'cope' with it."
Did you come up with—"handle" or "stand it" or "take it"?
"He was 'loath' to move in."
Did you use—"reluctant" or "hesitant"?
"He tried to 'foist' his ideas on the group."
Doesn't—"force," "impose," or "sell" speak better?
"There is a 'dearth' of talent."
Did you think of—"scarcity" or "lack of"?
By substituting words he might expect you give the listener a better chance of hearing what you said.

3. The Word He Doesn't Know

This group includes many words that the listener thinks he knows or words he gives a different meaning than you do.

The other evening in a panel discussion one man used the word "continuum" perhaps six or eight times. I did not know the word, and after the session I asked the man about it. He said, "I took thirty hours of Latin and that's the only thing I learned in the thirty hours."

He told me his meaning for the word. Later the president of the club gave the meaning he attached to it. The two definitions did not agree. My interpretation when he used this word was—outline—plan of action—pattern—but if he had meant any of these things, he would have done better to use the familiar word. The dictionary gives this definition—"continuum—something in which no parts can be distinguished from neighboring parts except by arbitrary division." Another dictionary gives it—"continuous quantity, series, etc." Tell me, please, did the man's thirty hours of Latin do him any good?

CHECK THESE WORDS

You might tell me that you never speak such words as—

rage
turgid
rapt.

A round of applause for you if you don't. If you know the meaning of and wanted to use those words, wouldn't it be better to use words the listener might hear because they are more familiar? Think of the selections you have—

for "rage," why not—"anger"—"fury"—"frenzy"—"madder than"?
for "turgid," why not—"swollen"—"bloated"—"inflated"?
for "rapt," why not—"absorbed"—"spellbound"—"carried away"?

You give your listener a better chance to hear with any of these words, and in most cases you can make your meaning clearer.

4. The Made-Up Words

It seems to me that all of us like to make up words. I have an acquaintance who says—"It's unclear." He means he doesn't understand.

Yesterday I heard—"maximated." Sounds as if this means—"built up"—"played up"—"inflated." If the word is new, one you have just heard, don't rush to use it. After a time, when more of us are using it, it has a better chance of being heard.

Trade names are in this group. You hear the pretty girl on TV say that her hair stays in place because there is XYZ in her hair spray. You don't hear the XYZ when she says it, and you probably wouldn't know what it was if you did hear.

Let's say your company makes a product with a trade name that doesn't explain itself. Use the trade name, but explain what it means. Here's how—

"This product is made with the famous Pluny process. Here's what the Pluny process is—"

You can't expect others to interpret your made-up words. Do it for them. If your trade name is not important, forget it. If it is important, explain it.

5. Words With a Negative Prefix

If you have the habit of using words with a negative prefix, it may be that the listener will hear just the opposite of what you say. Say—

"reporting is unnecessary"
and the listener may ask,
"How often do you have to report?"

Say—

"Reporting is not necessary"
and the listener may say,
"I like that."

In my book, "MAKING WHAT YOU SAY PAY OFF," I called this device "accentuating the negative." If you have the habit of using the negative prefixes, forget them. The listener has a better chance of hearing you if you make the negative more positive—

not "disallowed;" make that "not allowed"
not "irreplacable;" make that "not replacable"
not "misunderstood;" make that "not understood."

In a letter the reader has a chance to see those negative prefixes and he will understand, but when he listens, the latter part of the word may overshadow the prefix. Help him hear by not using negative prefixes.

6. Words With Modifiers

They fight each other—the word and the modifier. The listener may hear the adjective and not the noun, or it might be the other way around.

You say your enemy is a—"no-good so-and-so." Aren't all so-and-so's no good?

You say your friend is a—"polite gentleman." Aren't all gentlemen polite?

If the idea expressed by the adjective is important, give it a sentence, like this—"He's a so-and-so. He's also a crook." Say, "He's a crooked so-and-so," and the listener may ask, "He's a crooked what?"

In writing, the qualifying adjectives may help save space, but in speaking you strengthen your idea if you forget the modifier. Put the emphasis on the word you want to be heard.

How to Make Sure He Hears What You Say

You want the listener to hear what you say. If you use words in any of the categories listed in this chapter, you may be making it more difficult for him. He will stand for some difficulty, but not too much. You know what you do when you can't hear—you tune out, don't you?

Don't encourage listeners to tune you out.

Check the Words You Don't Hear

When you listen to radio or TV, try to figure out which words you don't hear. Was the word—

a short one
one you never heard
a made-up one
an unexpected one
overshadowed by a modifier?

This study will tell you the kind of words to avoid. If you stay clear of such words, others will hear what you say. Make it easier for those around you and they will help you move toward your TOP.

10

Helping Your Listener Understand

Say it in words he uses and he will understand. Think of the three requirements I listed for a word you speak.

The listener must—

hear it
know its meaning, and
give it the same meaning you do.

The listener's words rate 100 percent on those requirements. He will hear the word. He will know it, and in most cases he will know what you mean by it.

Why His Words Are Best

In speaking, it is your job to let the other know what you mean. You don't want him guessing, and he doesn't want to guess. If you use words he uses, you have a better chance of his understanding. His words are good because—

76

1. He Knows Them

You say to your boss, "This move will save us money." Those are familiar words. His mind starts asking how much, in what ways?

2. He Understands Them

When you use a word your listener does not know, he seldom asks, "What do you mean?" Let's assume your boss asks, "That's just conjecture, isn't it?" You may know what he means, but a lot of employees may not. The dictionary definitions offer these choices: guess—supposition. Your boss could have used a word that left no doubt.

3. They Make You His Kind of People

We have an affinity for those who speak our language. We prefer to go along with them. The one who uses different words than we do seems a different breed. We don't trust him as much as perhaps we should, but he generates the distrust by his choice of words.

Think of the Words to Describe a Person's Attitude

We could say he was—

cynical
perverse
arbitrary
truculent
gullible
dogmatic
credulous

By using any of those words we take a chance that the listener may not understand what we mean. Now check through these words—

optimistic
pessimistic

stubborn
negative
positive
headstrong

Each gives a clearer picture of the individual, doesn't it? And, if you use any from the second list, you are coming closer to the words your listener might use.

Talk Down—Talk Up

Executives tell me, "I don't believe in talking down to anybody." I agree, I don't either. I say, "Just speak the words he will understand."

Last Sunday I took a coloring book from my five-year-old granddaughter and started to draw a picture on one of the blank pages.

She watched me and asked, "What are you drawing, Grandad, an elephant?"

I said "No" and kept drawing.

Then, as the lines took shape, she cried, "Oh, Santa Claus—Ho, Ho, Ho."

That "Ho, Ho, Ho" indicated a meeting of minds. That "meeting of minds" comes easier when the other's words help clarify your meaning for him.

Don't Let Education Fool You

I questioned a college professor about a word he had used in a discussion with six of the junior executives in my company. "Why use such a word?" I asked.

He asked, "These men are all college graduates or equivalent, aren't they?"

They were all college graduates, but not in word knowledge. Too many finish college and have little more than a grade-school education in words. They never had any interest in vocabulary. You have probably read surveys that show top executives have larger vocabularies than men reporting to them. This may be true, but you gain nothing by trying to test your word knowledge when you speak to the brass of your company. Use words the boys in the back room will know. The brass will know them too.

Think of the Picture You Want the Listener to Have

You want him to picture you as you picture yourself—

a competent businessman
a good organization man
a responsible family man
a good fellow.

Add any other impression to that list. OK, we'll agree that is you. Now let's examine how the words you use can help build that picture.

Your Words Give You Away

You hear men speak on the radio or TV, you read reports of what they said in speeches. What they say gives you a picture of them—one a nobody, another ignorant, a third a stuffed shirt. This morning a big shot was quoted as saying—

"This is troglodytic thinking"

How many of the people you speak to would use that word? Not many, I'm sure. To express that idea, they would probably use—

cave-man thinking
old-fashioned thinking
out of touch thinking
obsolete thinking

You may protest, "I would never use a word like that." But if you did use a word like that, you would give your listeners a picture of the kind of person you are. Think of the kind of man you'd picture the other to be if he used that word in conversation with you.

If you are called on to tell others, who are not accountants, about a cost-cutting project you developed, use as little financial, accounting, or computer language as possible. You might be tempted to say—

"The savings will be minimal."

You are a financial man and the word is normal for you, but in this group there are many with no financial training. You will come closer to using their words if you say—

"The savings will be less than one tenth of a cent per part."

Every man on the committee would understand that. When you use the word "minimal," each member makes his own estimate of what "minimal" is.

Last night the football announcer on TV said—

"This was an auspicious break for the Giants."

He was speaking to a few million people.

If you were speaking to those people, what word would you use to describe the break?

Did you say—"lucky"?

It's the word most of us use with "break," isn't it?

Use the listener's words and there is no lack of communication.

Watch Phrases of Many Meanings

One of your friends says—

"I'm for educational reform."

You may agree—

"I am too."

But you can't be sure that you agree because he may be for certain reforms, and you may be for different reforms. You need to ask—

"What reforms are you for?"

When he answers, you can be sure if you agree or do not agree. Words of many meanings give this problem. "Easy" is a simple word. How many meanings can you think of for "easy?" Your dictionary gives at least seven—

not hard—it is an easy job.
requires little effort—easy payments
free from pain—resting easy
giving comfort or rest—take it easy
not harsh—easy on the complexion
not hard to influence—he'll go along easily
smooth and pleasant—the easy interview
not hard to get—he'll be easy to convince.

State your meaning when you use one of these words of many meanings. You may say, "When I say 'easy' he knows." Maybe yes, maybe no. Help him understand by explaining.

Check the People Around You

Some are easy to understand, others are difficult, right? If your listeners understand you, you have a better chance to reach your TOP.

11

Technicians, Please Translate Your Jargon

I have said that the learned are the most difficult to understand. You probably thought that I meant the highbrows. I did, but technical people are the ones that laymen hear most often. Thus I say to all you technically trained—

"Interpret your words"
"Tell us what you mean, please"

Use your technical words if you feel they give you stature, but when speaking to those of us not so educated, add—

"In laymen's language that means—"

Then explain in our words. You'll sound more like a human being if you do, like one of us. You'll make more friends, too.

The examples that follow show why this is important to: scientists—engineers—mechanics—medical men—dentists—religious—educators high and low—teachers—the military—lawyers.

Scientists, Engineers and Technical Men Can Build Character

While waiting for the go-ahead on the blast-off of Apollo 14, a scientist, in describing how they would compensate the flight angle because of the delay in starting, used a word that sounded like "asma." After he used it a number of times, Walter Cronkite broke in and asked, "What's an asma?" The man explained and went on with his description. I didn't hear the definition, and when I tried to find the word in the dictionary, I had no luck. Later, when I checked with an engineer friend, he said, "He probably used azimuth." He spelled it for me and I found the word in the dictionary. The dictionary says it is an astronautical term meaning the angular distance east or west from the north point. The azimuth of the North Star is zero degrees. The engineer said, "We'll change the azimuth." He told what would be done, but not too many listeners understood.

How to Translate Technical Words

Let's say you are a chemist and use the word—

sublimate

What thought does that bring to you?
My first definition was—residue.
Well, that's one of the definitions, but these are also given by the dictionary.

Sublimate—Chem—to purify—refine
Psychology—to divert the energy of primitive drives to behavior
          that is socially and ethically on a higher plane.
Chemical—material obtained when a substance is sublimed.

See why it helps to explain exactly what you mean?

How to Sell Your Ideas

In asking me to run a course for his men on "How To Sell Ideas," an engineering executive said, "We have lots of ideas, but

when we try to sell them to management, we fall flat on our faces."
He agreed that some of the ideas might be questionable, "But we
have to shelve so many, it's frustrating." "It's our language," another
said; "We can't make them understand."

One engineer said he had improved his performance by trying
to explain his ideas to his ten-year-old son. "I listen to the questions
the boy asks and try to change my approach to answer those questions." By simplifying his story so that the boy understood, he was
succeeding on more tries with his boss. This device can help any
technical man. If you have an idea to sell, explain it to somebody
without technical training—the wife, the youngsters, an acquaintance. Have them ask questions, and change your story on any part
that seems confusing.

How Medical Men Can Help Their Patients

Wouldn't you prefer a doctor who could explain clearly? Read
the letters to the physician who has a column in your newspaper and
you will see examples of how technical terms, difficult to understand,
can be clarified. In most cases the letter-writer had gone to his
physician and had been given a description of his ailment in technical words. Now the newspaper doctor explains what the terms
mean.

A physician friend told me that he was taking a course in public
speaking. I figured it was because he had been elected to the school
board, and I asked if that was the reason.

"Partly," he said, "but my wife gave me the big sell on it."

"How did she do that?" I asked.

"She told me, 'Anyone who hears you talk at those board
meetings might get the idea that you are not much of a doctor!' "

The doctor had all the practice he could handle, but since he
has been taking the course, he has been telling his patients the
technical name for what ails them, then adding, "In layman's language that means—" The patients who hear that second explanation
feel he is a better doctor. How is a patient going to explain to his
wife what ails him when his doctor uses words like: intervascular—
diuretic—hypertension—hemolysis—thrombolytic—paretial. They
all sound bad, but how bad?

Dr. George W. Crane, M.D., Ph.D, said, "If all the physicians could spend three months at door-to-door selling or serve an apprenticeship as a newspaper reporter, they'd soon learn to talk the language of the customer." And the customers or patient would go out of the offices knowing how minor or how serious his complaint is.

DENTISTS CAN CUT CONFUSION

Jim Bishop, the columnist, wrote a whole column on the confusing language that dentists use. One quote from a report started, "Due to furcation involvement—" You follow that, don't you? The report was written, but the D.D.S. stated that he had explained the condition to the patient. How? He had to go further than those words, didn't he? It would have helped if he had added—"in simpler language that means—"

How the Religious Can Save More Souls

If you listen to sermons every Sunday you may know of this need. You hear a clergyman speak of ideas we want to accept, but he makes a poor case for them.

One letter to a church newspaper said, "With the advances of this century in education, communication, and religious thinking, it would seem that church scholars would reach out to average men and women and give in laymen's terms the help to a better life." A friend told me he had stopped going to church. I asked why, and he gave as his reason, "That guy puts me to sleep."

A new church I pass every Sunday has hundreds of cars in its parking lot. I asked a member why they had such a large attendance and he asked, "Ever hear that preacher speak?" This man of God had apparently learned to speak a language that his listeners could understand. This is true all over the country—the preachers who can make sermons interesting draw great crowds.

Last week on TV I heard a man of the cloth dismiss a question with, "That is theopathetic thinking." Maybe it was, but what did he mean? Another cleric kept using the rather simple word, "secular." He would have been more understandable if he had used "worldly," or "not religious."

Educators Can Make a Better Impression

Just listen to a discussion by professors on TV and you'll get the idea that maybe there is a reason why your youngsters are having trouble on exams. You'll hear such gems as—

historical reductionism
linear planning
existential dilemma
middle-class parochialism
mind thrusts
sexual monism

You know the meaning of every one of those words. Every one, except perhaps "monism," is a word you might use. The learned can put two known words together and confuse you.

Translate this statement by a college president—"If we do not succeed in achieving a campus more voluntary than most of ours now are, if we do not restore a widespread faith in the openness of society, then our present troubles will seem as nothing compared to what lies ahead."

What do you think he means by a "campus more voluntary?" If you have an idea, try to say what you think he means in words easier to understand.

How do you interpret—"faith in the openness of society?" Try to say what you think he means in words easier to understand.

We all know what the word "voluntary" means, don't we?

We know—"faith"—"openness"—"society"—but the way he used those words leaves us confused.

Now try to put his statement in words that anybody would understand.

My guess is that you have clarified what the college president meant. From the words he used, he might have meant, "Turn the campus over to the students and the commie professors and let's see if that will save us from perdition."

Last night on TV a college professor said, "Genius has always been idiosyncratic." Do you know what "idiosyncratic" means?

Look it up and you'll find this or a similar definition—"a structural or behavioral peculiarity."

Now you understand. A genius has always been different. We

think of him as: eccentric—peculiar—a nut—crackpot—screwball. Think of a genius you know—which of these terms do you apply to him? If, instead of "idiosyncratic," the speaker had used any of these terms, all listeners would have understood, although the men of genius rating might not have liked the more popular descriptive word.

So hold it, Doctor, forget those far out words of yours, or please add the line, "In simple language that means—"

How Teachers Can Help Get the Votes They Need

One of my friends, Virginia Lee, a newspaper columnist, says that teachers, like teenagers, have come up with a vocabulary all their own. They use these fancy words with parents to discuss Junior's hang-ups in school. Here are some words she gives as examples: relevance—academic fluency—experience rating—comparability. For instance, "academic fluency" is what the old-timers called "book learning." Then you hear these teachers use—dialogue—laboratory—horizontal and vertical enrichment programs—social-living skills—curricular objectives. When I mentioned this to one teacher, he said, "Some use such words to intimidate the parents." The use of such words might give you a clue as to why voters are turning down levies to support the schools.

The Military Can Make a Better Impression

The military men have always been expert at using language that is difficult to understand. In a cartoon in the Cleveland Plain Dealer, the cartoonist drew the heads of two military officers and indicated they were carrying on this conversation—

"What is the justification for an incursion?"
"To interdict."
"What is it you interdict when you incurse?"
"Enemy supply routes."
"Following the conclusion of the interdiction, what is the evaluation?"
"Spectacular success."

There are four more questions and four more answers, but the ones quoted give you the idea. You hear such terms as "reinforced protection action" and you are told that this is different from "spontaneous protection action," and then you hear that there is another kind, "limited protection action."

It seems all technical people need that line—"In plain language that means—"

Lawyers Can Approach Clarity

The legal beagles hear many jokes about the language they use. One lawyer defended his legalistic terms with, "It's the kind of language that decisions are written in; we can't take a chance on clearer language." Another told me, "We have to learn it to pass the bar exams." OK, learn what you must, but in speaking to clients who did not study for the bar exams, translate your technical jargon. Do you assume that your client knows what you mean by "prima facie?" Don't be too sure. Make certain he does by using the line, "In layman's language that means—"

Technical Words Have Simple Substitutes

If you have a technical education and want listeners without that qualification to understand you, give your speech in your technical words, then add that phrase, "In simple language that means—" Now explain as simply as you can. If the explanation needs a simple sketch on a piece of paper to make it clear, draw the few lines.

TALK DOWN TO US

You won't hurt our feelings if you assume we don't know your specialized words. Tell us what you mean in plain "laymen's language" and you help us understand. In addition you increase our respect for you. The respect of others is a powerful ally in your march toward your TOP.

TIP TO NON-TECHNICALS

When you are greeted with any of the types of language reported in this chapter, ask your technician, "Would you, please, tell me exactly what that means?"

12

Management Words Won't Help You Climb

As you finish Chapter 11 you may say—"Technical people have trouble with words, don't they?"

Waste no sympathy on them. Non-technical businessmen have the same problem. Here is how they cut profits by using their favorites:

The boss uses words that aren't understood.

The junior executives use them.

Those aspiring to be junior executives use them, and the clouds of confusion spread.

The boss says, "We'll have to integrate it," or,

"We'd better compliment it," or,

"We'll need to implement it."

Maybe he knows what he means, but the junior executives and the workers start to "integrate," "compliment," or "implement" without knowing what the boss meant by the word.

These three words are what I call "grey area" words. They

mean one thing to one person, another thing to another person. The dictionary gives these definitions of "integrate":

complete
make into a whole
bring the parts together into a whole
indicate the total value
indicate the total amount.

The boss could explain more specifically, couldn't he?

Forget the Professor's Words

Much of this type of talk comes out of the business schools. Business sends its executives for refresher courses at the universities, and the executives come back to the job with some new words that the professors used.

One executive I worked with had just attended a two-month session on management at a University. As we worked together over a one-week period he mentioned the school a number of times, but he didn't need to tell me that he had been exposed to higher learning—I could tell by the terms he used. In describing one of his men he said, "He is an expert at group dynamics." Before the executive attended the school he might have said, "He runs a good meeting." That "group dynamics" was out of the mouths of his professors. Educators who use that term may protest, "That's not what 'group dynamics' means." Perhaps not when you use it, but how can you tell what it means when another uses it?

I believe it is good practice to send executives back to college for refresher courses. Most of them have not opened a book since they left school. The experience can't help but be of advantage to the men and their companies. It's unfortunate that they have to be exposed to the new words, but they are exposed—and they come back, start using them, and before long everybody is trying to use them.

Think of These Losses

Management jargon sounds impressive but if the employee doesn't understand specifically, you lose in many ways. For instance—

1. He lacks confidence. You may say, "He could ask what I meant." But you know he won't ask. That would make him appear dumb, and so he goes off to do the job. He wants to do it right, but without full understanding, if he does get it right, he is lucky.
2. The job isn't done right. That means it has to be done over, so time and effort, and perhaps material, has been lost.
3. The efficiency of your unit goes down; it becomes discouraged. You may alibi with, "I tell them and tell them," but if the mistakes go on, you are not telling them in the way you should.

Employees Rate You by Their Ability to Understand You

If your employee understands you, he feels you know what you are talking about. This is one reason why these management words are not helping get the job done.

In the Cleveland Plain Dealer, I read this comment about executive language: "The executives of big business use a tribal argot second only to insurance policies and income tax forms in its obsfucation."

The newspaper man is a student of words. If he finds the words of the business executive confusing, how can the man's employees determine their meaning?

You may say, "I'm not an executive yet; I don't use words like that."

I say, "Fine, don't cultivate the habit."

Don't be tempted by executives above you who use such words. Lay off them and give associates a better chance to understand what you mean.

Too Many Words Don't Tell It As It Is

Last month I made notes of these words spoken at a meeting of junior executives. Check through them—

marginal—pragmatic—segmentations—empirical—
dialogue—unstructure—fragmentation—unilateral—
methodology—functional—aggregate—catalizing—exploitation

—motivatee—consumerism—structured—pivotal—pilot—
entrepreneur—maturity—behaviorable—feedback—recall—
overview—actualization—conceptual.

You might say, "I know the meaning of every one of those words." But do you know what the speaker meant by them? You could say, "I would use such words only with a certain level of executives." That is a good idea, but read through that list of words again. Can't you express the meaning of any one of them in other words that would make your meaning clearer to your listeners? For each word listed you could have supplied a word or definition that was more specific, one that could be understood by almost anybody.

Blame It On Polarization

An executive I play golf with has found that he can stop his friends who want to ask worrisome questions about the war, taxes, environment, politicians, and other ills of the day with the comment, "I think we have to blame it all on this polarization that's going around today."

You might say, "Why, he isn't saying anything."

He isn't, as far as the listener's understanding is concerned. Most of the entries in that word list could produce almost the same result.

For instance—

"There's not enough implementation."
"We lack a catalizing force."
"Everything's too unilateral."

My friend's theory is that such a reply will confuse the one who wants to worry about the ills of mankind. It would confuse me, I'm sure However, it does get the subject changed, fast.

Don't Try to Talk Like a Manager

If you are not a manager, it can make you sound phony. If you °re a manager, it can make you sound high-hat.

Forget the new management words you hear. Give your speech

in words that leave no doubt of your meaning. Again, I advise, "Aim at making yourself clear."

If your employees understand you, the job gets done.

If your associates understand you, you get a reputation of getting along with the help.

If your social contacts understand you, you get a reputation as a good guy.

If your wife and kids understand you, you rate high where a high rating counts most.

Confusing management words never helped anyone get to the TOP.

13

How to Modernize Your Wording

Get with it.

I don't mean the youth speech of the day. I advise—reject the words and expressions our forefathers used in the Civil War period. Bring your wording up to today.

How Letter-Writers Have Done It

Most of us have taken a course in letter writing that has freed us from the stilted. We have learned to reject—

"Acknowledging your recent communication—"
"Enclosed herewith—"
"In response to your valued inquiry—"
"In reply to your favor of even date—"

The teachers called this "rubber-stamp" language. Through years of work much of it has been eliminated from business letters. The new language makes the writers seem more like human beings.

94

The teachers of letter writing told their learners, "You wouldn't say, 'In reference to your letter of even date, we regret to state;' then why write it?" Listen to the people who talk on TV, the amateurs and the pros, the educated and the uneducated, the washed and the unwashed. They are still using "war-between-the-states" words and expressions. The malaise takes three forms—

1. in words
2. in phrases, and
3. in the old stuffed shirt.

Your Words Date You

After certain words in the dictionary, the editors have placed the term *Arch.* to show that it is archaic. These are not the words I refer to. In the sentences that follow, the word underlined helps date the speaker. Change these sentences by subsituting another word for that dated word and note how you give life to the sentence.

The plan was *fraught* with danger.
To what do you *ascribe* its success?
I tell you in all *candor.*
He belonged to the *dissident* group.
It is a *flagrant* offense.
There is a *paucity* of evidence.
The group showed nothing but *apathy.*
I was *remiss* in my duty.
We need *stringent* rules.
He seemed *affluent.*
We had no *recourse.*
It was a *dismal* showing.
He showed his *acumen.*
We tried to *assuage* his anger.
I don't *perceive* that result.
The fraud was *perpetrated.*
They didn't *preclude* flying.
He had no *qualms* about it.

You had no trouble, did you? You know more modern words; why use the words that make you seem old-fashioned?

You may ask, "Where did you get that list of words?" I heard them spoken on TV. As you looked them over, you supplied the meaning of each in more modern language. I consider all of them poor for speaking. My advice is, don't say—

"The miscreant pilfered the bicycle."
He stole it, didn't he?

Don't say—

"The culprit rifled the cash drawer."
He took the money and everything else, didn't he?

Maybe you'd say—

"He cleaned out the till."

I am sure that what you propose would be more modern than the original.

OLD-FASHIONED WORDS MIGHT INDICATE OLD-FASHIONED THINKING

We think with words.

If our words are old-fashioned, might not the listener assume that it would be difficult to get us to accept anything but an old-fashioned idea? You know a person who uses the type of words given in the examples. How do you rate him?

2. Your Phrases May Give the Wrong Picture

When I mention a "cliché," you think of the oldies such as, "A penny saved is a penny earned." It is surprising how often a cliché of this type pops into our minds when we want to express a thought. You hear many of them on TV. Next time you hear one, note the look of satisfaction that comes over the face of the speaker when he comes up with a gem like, "A stitch in time." His manner indicates that he has scored with a bright saying.

These ancient expressions seem to be both handy and comforting. I advise you to cut such expressions, but it is not these that I am speaking against—it is those that follow. As you read each of these tired expressions, substitute words that would bring them up to the language of today.

I don't give credence to it.
He was the cynosure of all eyes.
He drank copius quantities.
The drive succeeded in surpassing its goal.
The idea merits serious consideration.
It behooves us all.
The activity will gain momentum.
A motley crew.
We ask your continued support.
I won't belabor the point.
Are you cognizant of any effort to make the rules uniform?
It becomes increasingly apparent.
It will take strong and effective measures.

Football is modern, but how would you change this wording which the announcer used the other evening—

The tackle and the linebacker collaborated on the stop.
Duke sustained an ankle injury in the first quarter.
The ball came to rest in the grasp of Archie.

I warn against the use of such wording because an individual on his way to the TOP needs more modern speech.

When asked if he had pursued a certain subject in school, Charles A. Brower, a leading advertising executive, answered, "I have indeed pursued it, and in some cases nearly caught up with it."

3. Beware Of The Old Stuffed Shirt

None of us think of ourselves as a stuffed shirt. We're ordinary follows—today's type of good guys, or at least we're trying to be. In one of my sessions an executive asked, "What is your definition of a stuffed shirt, Ed?" I seldom answer a question like that. It goes up for discussion. It was agreed that a stuffed shirt was a person whose words and manner indicated that he wasn't a part of the current scene, a guy who wasn't quite with it, who spoke in the language of the 1890's. I asked, "Do any of you consider yourself a stuffed shirt?" Strange, but nobody felt he rated as such. There follow some words a stuffed shirt might use. Try to modernize each. Start with these favorites that supervisors use when introducing speakers to meeting groups

> pay strict attention
> heed this beneficial advice

> Now try to modernize these—

> I solicit your earnest cooperation
> It was felt preferable not to quarrel
> I hope all of you will seek to emulate
> I wish to express my gratification
> I'd be lax in my responsibility if
> We are embarking upon this plan
> This is a sincere manifestation
> The drive has made substantial progress

I am sure that the way you express the idea is more up to date. Why speak in antebellum language in these days of nuclear power?

When you hear a stilted remark on the TV tonight, put it in modern words. This exercise is fun to try, and you'll gain by following it.

Add Life to a Statement by Using More Modern Language

At a flag football victory dinner the other evening one of the fathers told the boys,

> "You must put forth the best efforts of which you are capable to maintain the position which you have achieved."

What does that statement show?
How about this—

a generation gap
a speaker a bit behind the times
a wordy statement that could be shortened.

Yet this is how we foul up. The youngsters hearing that bit think, "Just like my dad." And they go away a bit more convinced that no adult understands them or their problems.

Check This Effort of Mine

How about expressing that thought to the team this way—
"Give it all you've got, and you'll stay in first place."
You may never be asked to talk to a group of youngsters, but if you are, try to speak naturally to them. Remember, they think of you as an ancient, anyway.

Let the Past Stay Past

Using the language of years ago has another fault—it can be misunderstood. You might be surprised, as was the personnel man who was interviewing an applicant for a job and asked, "What is the length of your residence at the present address?"
The applicant thought a minute and said, "About fifty-two feet."
Why didn't the man ask—

"How long have you lived at this address?"

You Gain by Modernizing

As you listen to TV, you'll hear many phrases that could stand modernizing. Try putting these in more modern words. Such exercises will help you avoid such language. It will stop you from using many phrases that you use today. The change in your language helps because—

Your bosses notice it
Your associates notice it
Your social contacts notice it
You seem more up to date to them.

Ask yourself, "How can I say it to make me seem more alive and alert?"

Alive and alert talk gives the impression that the speaker should be up at the TOP.

HAVEN'T YOU NOTICED IMPROVEMENT?

Most of the devices mentioned in Part Three of this book are easy to try out. They are so easy that I am sure you have tried some of them. The ones you used have helped you show improvement in the effectiveness of your speech, haven't they? Perhaps you haven't tried some that would help more. Check through this list to see. Haven't—

you stopped speaking words from your written vocabulary
you used words that were easier to hear
you helped the listener understand by using words he might use
if you are a technical man, you added, "In layman's language that means—"
you've given up the idea that management words made you sound more like a manager
you've discarded some old-fashioned ways of saying things?

Of course you didn't need to use every one of them, but you tried enough of the devices suggested to prove that they help. Keep on using these ideas. The ones you have already read and the ones coming up will help you move ahead faster.

Part IV

HOW TO KEEP YOUR BIG MOUTH FROM HOLDING YOU BACK

All of us have faults in speaking.

Every day you hear others around you speak in a way that holds them from promotion. You feel that if you had such an obvious fault you would do something about correcting it.

If you are sincere in that, here is a challenge. Each chapter in this part of the book discusses a speaking fault that gives listeners a bad impression of you. Most of us who have these faults don't know we have them. The chapters in Part Four tell you how to check to see if you have the fault, then how to correct it easily and permanently.

The challenge—check to see if you have the fault, and if you have it, work to correct it.

If you find that you have none of the objectional faults mentioned, hooray for you. But check, please, before you respond to the applause.

14

How to Talk Less and Say More

You know fellow workers who have the habit of spending more time talking about a job than it would take to get the job done. With their yak-yak they are handicapping themselves.

In business, decisions are wanted, not dissertations. Once my boss said to me, "Let's decide this without talking to Charlie; he'll want to talk all morning about it."

In organizations, the same is true. You have heard the club member stall the meeting by his desire to argue about a silly change in the by-laws. No one else is interested, but he wants to talk—and he does—while you decide you'll not vote for him for any office.

At home, members of the family won't bring up certain subjects because they don't want to hear the speaker talk and talk about them.

How to Check Yourself on This Fault

Here are some checks you might make to see if you have even a trace of this habit.

102

Review Your Day

Ask yourself who does the most talking—

in your share-the-ride club
at the coffee breaks
at lunch
in the department meetings.

If the answer is "I do," you may be losing friends.

Check The Other's Attention

If your listener indicates in any way that he is not listening, stop talking. This will bring his attention back to you. Maybe you have said enough on the subject. Ask a question to check if he has heard enough, such as—

"Want to hear more details?"

Check What He Told You

I suggest this idea with salesmen. When a conversation with a customer is finished, I suggest the salesman sit in the car and figure out what he was told.

What ideas did the customer offer?
What suggestions did he make?
Did he suggest I consult others?

This idea can be used on any conversation. If you remember little the other said, maybe you talked too much.

How We Waste Words

The examples that follow illustrate the faults of the individual who dominates the conversation. Even though you don't rate in this class, you might have other excess-talk faults. Check through this list.

WE USE TOO MANY WORDS

If you make notes of statements you hear on TV, you'll record many examples of the speaker using too many words. You hear the man being interviewed say—

"He actually threatened me."

That word—"actually"—is not needed. You will hear many of this kind of word: literally—relatively—generally—basically—frankly—primarily—incidentally—historically—practically—categorically—parenthetically.

Another type of excess is the introduction: in fact—in effect—in substance—in other words.

If you have the habit of using any of these expressions, streamline your speech by dropping them.

You hear the man say—

"I was in the process of backing the car out."

He was backing the car out, wasn't he?

You may protest, "All I save is three words." That is all—three words. But that's an easy way to cut overtalk—a few words at a time. Remember, most improvements come a bit at a time.

INTRODUCTIONS ADD WORDS

While the one- and two-word introductions mentioned waste a word, too many waste more words. You'll hear the man being interviewed on TV say—

"The answer to that is simply this—"

Couldn't he have answered without the preliminary words? He probably could have, but this is one way he overtalks.

ADD-ONS ADD WORDS

On TV you'll hear gems like—

"an attempt to appease appetites, wills, interests, and aspirations"

The man tried to say it all, didn't he? Why say "means and methods" when perhaps one would do. We say, "facts and figures and things like that." We'd do better if we said, "The facts show," or "The figures indicate." It is better to forget the "things like that." If you have this habit of using doubles or triples, try to correct it.

Take This Advice from a Sixth Grader

My grandson, Mike Hegarty, when he was in the sixth grade, was scheduled to be in a debate, the subject of which was, "Should patent medicines be outlawed and taken off the market?"

He had the negative side. His mother told me about the debate and I asked him if I could be of help.

"No," he said, "we've got the best guys on our side."

I asked, "How about the arguments?"

"We've got the best arguments, too."

"Mind telling me what they are?"

"No—if the only medicine you could get was the medicine the doctors prescribe, medicine would cost more." I asked for his other arguments. He said,

"That's all we are going to use, just one. These kids will understand that one."

These youngsters in the sixth grade understood a principle that many grown-up speakers never learn. You don't need four or ten arguments to win a debate. If one is strong enough, you can win with that.

Yes, Mike's side won.

LOADED QUESTIONS ADD WORDS

The long question is an example of too much talk. In my speech sessions I have tried to limit questions from those attending to ten words. Mighty few of the men can observe this rule.

Ten words seem enough, but they aren't. In a small department meeting I heard this question—

"Why did we adopt this policy—to appease the unions, to save face for the management, to pacify the office workers, or to please the customers?"

The employee completed his question in the first six words. The added words seemed to be an attempt to show that he understood what might have brought on the policy.

If he was interested particularly in one of the reasons he suggested, he could have asked, "Did we do this to appease the union leaders?" By including everything, he was indicating that he wanted to show off.

You see this in the news conferences of the President on TV. Not one of the questioners seems to be able to ask a question in less than fifty words.

Check yourself on this skill. Next time you ask your boss a question, count the words you use. The assistant who can ask questions in a few words will be rated higher.

How to Stop Talking Too Much

Here are some ideas that others have used to achieve more brevity in their speech.

1. Ask Others

Ask your supervisor, friends and associates if they feel you talk too much. If they indicate you might, ask in what way. If the answers to your questions indicate that you overtalk, try one of these remedies.

2. Limit Any Group Discussion

I had a supervisor who talked over plans with his group. When he felt we had talked enough, he asked, "Haven't we talked enough on this?" Usually he got agreement. Then he would say, "Let's each of us get back and work on his part." When I complimented him on this idea, he said, "They'd talk all morning if I let them."

3. Listen Twice As Long As You Talk

One man in my speech clinic told me that he had cured himself of talking too much by trying to give others twice as much time to speak as he took. I once had an assistant who talked too much on any subject. My supervisor couldn't take it and he told me to fire the man. The assistant was a most efficient worker except for this yak-yak habit. I told the boss this and after much argument he agreed, "OK, you can keep him, but you have to get him to keep his mouth shut, especially around me." I talked out the problem with the assistant and we agreed that whenever he was in a meeting with the boss, he would remain silent unless he was asked for an opinion.

4. Talk a Bit, Then Pause

One manager suggested this plan: "The pause indicates that now it is time for the other guy to talk," he said. "Does it work?" I asked. "Great. It has shown me that others want to talk, too."

5. Cut the Answers to Questions

I mentioned the idea of cutting the length of questions to ten words. Cut the answers short, too. If "yes" or "no" is enough, why elaborate? Most question and answer sessions are marred by answers that run on and on.

6. One Point at a Time

Try to include a number of points in one statement and you can confuse listeners. Let's say you argue that the proposed move is against tradition, that it really won't improve conditions, and that the club doesn't have the money to make the move. The first two reasons may be open to argument, but that third can't be ignored. Stay with the main point, and ignore the others.

GIVE LISTENERS A BREAK

The jokester says, "Speech is free; perhaps that's why there is so much of it." The other day, during the broadcast of the football game, the audio was lost for a few minutes. The announcer said, "I just learned the audio was lost. Maybe that was a break for you." His "you" meant the millions listening. He meant it as a joke, but perhaps a high percentage of those listeners agreed it was a break to be allowed to see the action in silence.

Give your listeners a bit of that silence so they can get in a few words and you'll speed your way toward your TOP.

15

How Good Talk Habits Help You Climb

Develop talk habits that show you are—

alive
alert
full of vim, vigor, enthusiasm
competent.

All around you there are people with bad speech habits that make a poor impression. If yours are good, you get noticed.

Check your speech habits that help others form opinions about you. Every one of them can hold you back. Better news is that all can be easily corrected. How about—

Greetings

How do you think your boss appraises your brain power if you greet everybody with—

"How's tricks?"
    or
"What do you know?"

You may say, "I don't use such inane greetings." Good for you, but what greeting do you use? Think of associates who always greet you with a silly greeting. Too many, aren't there? Most of us would do better with, "How are you today?"

The one so greeted may tell you he is okay or has a crick in his neck, but he doesn't rate you as shy in intelligence.

THINK OF THE FIRST IMPRESSION

Your greeting gives the other his first impression of you. It tells him how the day is going for you. Plan it to give a good impression. Even though you greet someone every day, let your greeting help show him that you are glad to be alive, you're ready to do a full day's work, and have the energy to do it. If your greeting shows you are dragging, how can you make a good impression?

Same Closing

You meet a friend on the street, you converse a few minutes, you depart and close the contact with—

"Take care"
    or
"Take it easy."

I heard one friend tell a man who admonished him to take it easy, "The United States of America was not built by men who took it easy."

"Burns me up," he told me, "those silly bits of advice."

Many of us don't notice such parting bits, but others do. We can be safe with all by using a few words of well-wishing. Why not, "Good luck to you." The friend may say, "Same to you" or "Likewise," but you have ended your conversation on a friendly, personal note.

Same Designation

Many of us have the irritating habit of using one word over and over. One of my bosses told me, "I wish you wouldn't call everybody a 'guy.'" I didn't know I was doing that, but after he reminded me, I was surprised at how often I used the word. Look at the words available to indicate a man: brother—character—companion—comrade—fellow—buddy—associate—neighbor—chap—chum—crony—pal—colleague. I'm sure that as you read those choices you thought of other words that could be used. Our language gives us thousands of choices, yet we use one word over and over. To break this habit, I started calling every man a "fellow"—"This fellow asked me." "This fellow showed me how." If you substitute "fellow" for "guy" half of the time, you have improved your speech.

The Same Modifier

I had an assistant who used the word "tremendous" to describe how everything was going. It was always—

"tremendous idea"
"tremendous cooperation"
"tremendous success"

The young man's choice of words showed his enthusiasm, but he was overusing that word.

This choice of "tremendous" is similar to the exaggerated claims you hear in TV advertising. Once in a while "tremendous" would be all right, but the listener knows that everything can't be "tremendous." The assistant could have used: good—great—super—beautiful—exciting—brilliant—unusual—outstanding—appealing—splendid—bold—wonderful.

As you look over those substitutes, you might say, "I wouldn't use some of those words to describe an idea." Maybe, you wouldn't, but aren't there three or four that you might use? I made up the list to show that for any modifier there are many substitutes to express the idea, and there is no need to use one favorite.

My choice from that list would be—

"good idea"
"fine cooperation"
"unusual success"

Each of the substitutes sounds more believable, and they wouldn't have attracted any attention. Any attention drawn to your words rather than your meaning hinders your communication.

The Same Expression

Younger children drive a baby sitter crazy with a question, asked hundreds of times during one sitting job, "You know what?" A small girl who came in to see the Christmas decorations at our house kept saying as we showed her around, "Oh, that's cute." Youngsters will grow out of those habits, but some of us don't seem to. Many people use these—

"Think of that"
"For cryin' out loud"
"That's the way the ball bounces"
"You can't figure some people"
"Are you putting me on?"
"You'd better believe it"
"What do you know about that?"

Ask your wife or an associate if you have any such expression that bothers her or him. If you have, change the words to ask something about what he is discussing, for instance—

"Is this the brother-in-law out in Jersey?"

Such a question shows interest in what he is telling you. He will like that.

Cut The Familiar "You Know"

How many times will you say these words tomorrow? Everybody seems to have taken on the habit. The man in the street interviewed on TV, the public official, it seems anyone speaking without a script uses it. Within the next hour you'll probably use it in explaining something to somebody. You'll say something like, "I was walking down Main Street (you know) and I stopped to look in Burg's Furniture Store window (you know) and saw this beautiful lamp on a table (you know)."

We use the expression like a punctuation mark. It adds nothing but words to the story we are telling. I find it slipping into my conversation and I have been trying for months to break myself of the habit. Check your speech for any such expression you use over and over.

The Same Cliché Over and Over

Too many of us think in clichés. Too often in speaking we come up with an oldie such as—

"A blind pig—"

Try putting that into your own words. You supplied the words for that very quickly, didn't you. Put all such thoughts in your own words in this way—

for "a stitch in time"
why not—be prepared?
for "strike while the iron is hot"
how about—do it immediately?
for "hit the nail on the head"
what do you think of—that's exactly right?

Five Easy Steps to Better Speech Habits

1. Put some life into your greeting and parting words. Your first tries will show improvement, but with continued practice you will get so good that your associates will realize you mean what you say. If possible, make the greeting and parting words personal.
2. Get a few new words for individuals.
3. Add a few new modifiers.

4. If you have a favorite expression, give it a rest.

5. Then, if you use any clichés, put the idea into your own words. The listener will understand the thought expressed by the cliché, but he may rate you by it.

Check yourself on these common speech faults. All are rather easy to correct. All offer big improvements on the impression you make on others. Without the faults, you will increase your chances of reaching your TOP.

16

How You Can Dodge the "No" Man Tag

John Salisbury, Portland news analyst, nominates as one of America's major afflictions—

the abominable "no" man

You say, "Let's—" to such a character and he answers, "Let's not—." You say, "Hey, here's an idea," and he says, "It won't work." Everytime you say "yes," he says "no."

You find him everywhere—in families, companies, clubs—even in high places in politics. John asks, "Doesn't he know—can't he learn that—'no' man's land is a wasteland where nothing can grow?"

Check How You Rate as a "No" Man

You may say, "I don't rate in that class." Do you think the man you rate as a "no" man thinks he could be called a "no" man? Just make this check on yourself by answering these questions about the type of talk you do every day—

How Do You Respond to Greetings?

What do you answer a friend who greets you with—

"How are you?"

Do you say—

pretty good
could be better
sorry you asked
not so hot?

If so, you have warned this greeter that you belong to the family of "no" men, and why should he want to continue talking with you?

Do You Accept News with Approval?

You hear at lunch that Pete's wife has won an all-expense-paid trip for two to Hawaii. One of the group says, "Lucky stiff." You say—"With his brains he better be lucky." That's "no" man language and those that hear rate you as such. Say, "That's great, isn't it?" That's "yes" man. Say, "I'd like to win a trip like that myself," and you are still a "yes" man. Whenever you hear of a break, a promotion, or a success, applaud. Don't allow your big mouth to rate you as a negative.

How Do You Talk About the Ideas of Others?

Let's say another explains an idea to you. Would you ever say—

"It won't work"
     or
"The boss won't go for it"
     or
"Your wife won't agree?"

If you use these or similar words, you are a "no" man to the man with the idea. Say 'tell me more" and you're OK.

How Do You Give Advice?

One of your associates asks your opinion of buying one of the new small cars the American manufacturers have put on the market. Would you tell him—

"I wouldn't do that; wait until they get some experience with them."

That makes you a "no" man, doesn't it? Even though that is your honest opinion and you believe it is what the man should do.

What's Your First Reaction?

When you hear of a new project of your company, club, or city fathers, what is the first reaction you put into words? Is it for or against? If it is negative, those who hear you voice that opinion may rate you as a "no" man.

How Do Others Approach You?

If you are the one who makes decisions, do those who come to you indicate that they think it would be difficult to get you to say "yes?" I was working as a consultant with a group on the introduction of a new product, and the proposal we were to make to the president suggested that a certain part of the product would be "pink." I said, "I don't think that part should be pink." The man working with me said, "Neither do we, but we know that if we say pink, the boss will say pink is no good. Then we'll show him this green we really want. He will say, 'Now you're talking.' " That is one way of handling "no" men. I saw it used, and the scheme worked. How much do you think that president lost by his "no-no" attitude?

A man in my speech session told about his wife approaching him on a project with, "I know you'll be against this—"

He asked, "Why do you know I'll be against it?"

"You're against anything that costs money," she answered.

If anyone approaches you with such a statement, you have earned yourself a reputation as a "no" man with them.

If your answer to any of these questions indicates that you lean toward being a negative, there follow some ideas on how to get on the opposite side.

How to Change to the Positive Side

1. Use a Positive Response to Greetings

When the other greets you with "How are you," say—

"great"
"fine"
"couldn't be better"

Small improvements help you move up step by step.

2. Cheer the Good Luck of Others

When you hear that another has had a break, a windfall, or a success, join in the celebration; tell everyone that you are glad, that he deserves it.

3. Develop Some Positive Statements

Instead of rushing to say that an idea won't work, say such things as—

"This might have a chance."
"It is a new approach."
"Maybe you've got something there."

The words need not be 100 percent positive, but they should tend to encourage.

4. Listen to Ideas and Ask Questions

Try this two-step plan and you won't be rated as a "no" man. First, listen to the idea, let him tell you all he wants to tell. Second, show interest by asking questions about it. His answers can tell you how thoroughly he has covered all angles. They can also indicate to him that he needs to check certain points.

5. Offer to Help

When you have listened to an idea, an offer to help takes you out of the "no" man class. You might ask—

"What facts can we use to sell the boss on this?"
    or
"How can we strengthen your presentation?"

Note the "we" in these questions. The questions indicate that the idea has a chance, even though it needs some more work.

6. Ask, "What's My Real Reason for Being Negative?"

Many times, your reaction to a proposal has nothing to do with its value. You don't like the fellow who made it, or you are competing with him for the job ahead and you don't want to see him get credit for anything. Don't be against the idea because of any such reason. By being negative you give your opponent the opportunity to say, "Hank's pretty much against anything new."

7. Say Something Good

You have heard the advice, "If you can't say something good, say nothing." If your first reaction is negative, ask yourself, "What's good about it?" Then make a list of the good points. If you dwell on the negative, you'll think of more reasons against. If you start listing the good points, you'll push the negatives into the back ground.

8. Say "That's Good" More Often

You can't go through life approving everything, but there is no sense in knocking everything either. Assume that you are tempted to say, "That's no good." Instead, ask a question about the idea. Such a policy will help you with the people at the office, your social contacts, and your wife and children. One of my friends has a sign on his office wall that reads—

WE NEVER SAY "NO" HERE

You don't need a sign, but try that idea for a while.

Who Wants "No" Men?

Why should business want executives who always see the negative side? Business wants new ideas, new approaches. Times keep changing, and business must change to keep pace.

Why should your club promote the fellow who is always against change? The club wants new members or more prestige, and it can't get what it wants by holding the status quo.

Why should your family be enthused about the head man who always says "no?" You can't run a happy home with a "whatever they ask, say no" policy.

Some "No's," Yes, but Not Always

Some "no's" are called for. Don't run from them. But try using some of the devices mentioned to add that touch of finesse that helps keep friends even when you must say "no." One of my friends described an associate thus: "He's always sweeping the sunshine under the rug."

If such a statement can be made about you, you may be keeping yourself away from that TOP you have selected.

17

Why It Pays to Let the Other Fellow Be Right

Now and then, at least.
Think of a friend or associate whose words indicate—

"I am always right"
"I was never wrong"

He annoys you, doesn't he?
Are you of this type? If you have even a slight touch of this affliction, you are cutting yourself off from information or advice that could help. Think how much positivity you hear.

Listen to the Advertisements

The automobile dealer says—

"No deal refused"

121

Do you believe that?
Or another dealer's statement—

"You make your own deal"

Then you hear—

"My pain reliever is more effective than Brand X."
"My cold remedy cleans sinuses cleaner."
"My detergent makes clothes whiter than other detergents."

You don't believe any of these claims, do you? Mainly because the man who states them seems to be too right.

IT'S ALL AROUND YOU

You hear this type of over-positive talk from—

politicians—commentators—protagonists—campus agitators—the rightists—the leftists—revolutionaries—conservatives—progressives.

They all tell you, "You have to do something right now, or the gates of hell will open for you."
They probably never read the poem that I found in a newspaper years ago—

"We shun the man who's always right,
Who sounds off morning, noon and night.
Listeners class him with other nuts,
And one and all just hate his guts."

There is a lot of truth in that bit. If your talk indicates you are always right, why wouldn't others think that way about you?

Check Yourself on This Liability

Here are some questions you can use to check yourself on this fault that one of my friends calls "pregnant positivity."

1. Do Others Let You Talk On?

One of the men in my speech clinic said, "I have an associate who is always right."

"How do you work with him?" I asked.

"I let him talk; I never disagree with him. I guess I just tune out."

"Would you operate more efficiently if you both talked?" I asked.

"Sure, but you can't do it with that guy."

If others let you yak on, without ever putting up an objection, don't assume it is because you are right. It may be because they don't want to start an argument.

2. Do You Alibi Much?

Somewhere I read, "The alibi is just an attempt to prove that you weren't wrong." It may be good to review why the mistake occurred so that you might guard against making the same mistake again, but the harm is done and you can't help by trying to get out from under the blame. If you have the habit of trying to justify every mistake, you can be rated as one who always has to be right.

3. How Do You Accept Advice or Criticism?

If you listen to it, you rate well; if you ask questions about it, you rate better; if you thank the advisor for it, you are tops. If, instead, you try to explain why you are doing the job your way or why you think your way is best, you are discouraging others to try to help you in any way.

4. How Long Since You Admitted a Mistake?

Do you ever admit you are wrong? If you can't remember when, you may be leaving an impression on others that you feel you can't make a mistake. I was working for a small unit of a large corporation that was closed out. The news was a surprise because we thought we were doing a good job of getting the unit started. When my boss gave me the sad news, he asked, "Can you figure where we goofed up?" Notice he blamed us. It shows he was big enough to admit he was at fault, or that some of the fault was his.

Why Positivity Is Easy to Correct

If you have any one of the faults mentioned, it is not too difficult to correct them. Men tell me, "I believe in positive thinking." That's fine, but being right all of the time is not positive thinking. Think positively about yourself. You're competent. You've got many good qualities. You're a good provider. There is nothing wrong about that kind of thinking, but it is so easy to handle talk situations in a way that indicates you are not always right. Try these ideas—

Use Questions Instead of Opinions

Let's say an associate tells you about an idea he has. You comment—

"It will take too much time."
"You can't do it for less than twenty bucks."
"Your assumption is pure nonsense."

Such comments indicate that your opinions are too positive.
Note the difference when you handle your comments in questions such as these—

"How much time do you think it will take?"
"What do you estimate it will cost?"
"Does that assumption make good sense to you?"

You are asking, not telling. The reason we don't like the one who is always right is because he keeps telling us, not asking us.

Forget Alibis

In most cases they waste time. Remember the time you tried to explain how a mistake occurred, and your supervisor said, "OK, forget that, let's get on to correcting the damage."
An alibi satisfies nobody. Listeners don't need it, and you don't

believe it. Stop looking for someone or something to blame for any mistake. Maybe there were extenuating circumstances, but forget them. Nobody ever got promoted because he is an artist at alibiing.

Take Advice With Thanks

When another offers suggestions on how to do a task, listen to his idea and ask questions about it. Don't try to explain why you think another way is better. You know how you feel when another asks your advice, you give it, and he says, "Oh, that won't work at all." Listen to the advice, ask questions about it, and thank the other for it.

Learn From Criticism

Nobody likes criticism, but when you hear any that reflects on your work, listen to it without showing your feelings. Ask questions about what the man says. If you start to justify your action that brought on the criticism, the critic is inclined to say, "This guy doesn't want any help."

Try "I Had That Trouble"

A device used by supervisors to discuss mistakes with employees is the admission, "I once had that trouble and here's how I corrected it." Let's say a young employee has the fault of calling all of the big executives by their first names. You know that certain big shots will not be overjoyed by this, and you want to get the young man to use "Mister" with these men. You explain how you taught yourself to do this.

Note the plan here—if you say that you once had this trouble, you are admitting that you were not always right, that you had to learn.

Assume Partial Responsibility for Employees' Mistakes

If you are a supervisor and a mistake has been made by one of your group, forget questions such as—

"Why didn't you check this?"
"How did you get yourself in this spot?"

Each of those questions indicates that the fault was wholly with the one who made the mistake. Change those two questions to indicate that you, the department, or the company share the blame.

For instance—

Was there any way to check this?
What do you think we should do the next time this situation arises?

The employee will still feel that he goofed, but he appreciates you for taking some of the blame. We all like the boss who backs us up.

Say "It Was My Fault" More Often

Add these words to your vocabulary—

"I goofed"
"I fouled it up"
"I was wrong"

Those who hear the words usually know who is at fault anyway. By using them you'll make more friends and demonstrate that you are a better manager. In one of my sessions a young man said, "The only fellow who has to be right all of the time is the guy who works on the high trapeze without a net." At most jobs, the employee doesn't have to be that right.

A poet has said, "None but a fool thinks he is always right." Imitating the fool won't help you reach your TOP.

18

The Right Attitude Helps

Those who hear your words expect them to show the right attitude about—

your work
your business
the brothers at the lodge
your family and friends.

If what you say shows that you don't have what they call the RIGHT attitude, they rate you lower than you may deserve.

Eight Ways to Show the Right Attitude

Here are eight ways to let your words help show the attitude that others rate as right:

1. Speak As If You Like Your Work

Yesterday I heard a man say—

"These slave-drivers I work for."

Do you think less of the company or the speaker?
Do you refer to your company management as—

"They" or "we?"

You perhaps have long-time employees around your work place
who speak as if they owned the company, yet they are on minor jobs.
They say "we" or "us" or "our." Take a tip from them. Show you
feel you belong. Let your words show—

you like your job
you think your company is tops
you like its policies
its employees are the greatest.

Whenever you hear a man make depreciatory remarks about
his job or company, don't you wonder why he doesn't look for
another job?

2. Associate With the Other's Problems

The individual who moves up understands the problems of his
fellow workers.

One executive I worked with gave me this assignment: "This
young fellow I have running errands for me rubs my managers the
wrong way. See if you can find out how he makes them sore."

I talked with the young man and thought he had promise. I
made two calls with him and found his trouble. He would take the
message to the department head and say, "Mr. Boss wants this data."
His manner indicated, "You'd better get it, and fast."

I suggested he change his approach to, "How much trouble will
it be to dig out this data for Mr. Boss."

Such a question is in line with the manager's first thought, the
extra work in digging out the information. If the manager's answer
indicated a lot of work, the young man could say, "If it is that much
trouble let me go back and ask if the information is that important."

The young man changed his approach, and when I met him

six months later he said, "The managers have taken me into their lodge." The top man asked, "What did you do to him?" All I did was suggest he use words that indicated he was thinking of the other's problem. Think the same thoughts the other is thinking, and he sees that you are on his side.

3. Let Others Work With You, Not For You

I asked a vice president of a large corporation if he knew an acquaintance of mine who worked for his company. He answered, "Do I know him? I'm his boss, he works for me."

What did that reply tell me about the V.P.?

A neighbor told me about his pal who was made his boss.

"He wants us all to call him 'Mister,' " he complained. "Before he was Mike; now that he has joined the brass, he wants all of us to bow low."

You can imagine how the help felt about this attitude. The boss didn't make him a king, he only put him in charge.

Avoid Mike's mistake. If you are made a supervisor, don't move in with big talk that glorifies your importance. You are not important. If your group doesn't come through, you won't hold the job too long. If you indicate you are better than members of your group, you won't do too well with them. Talk about: our group—our department—our team—our performance. Use "we"—we can do it—we're the best. Use "us"—nobody can beat us. If you are asked about an employee, say "He works with me." Maybe you are his boss, but if you mention that fact, don't you sound as if you are bragging?

4. Never Question Intelligence

My boss and I were supervising the recording of a sound track for a film. It was difficult for the announcer because of the technical language involved. He stumbled; we went back, made corrections and continued. When the director, after hours of work, approved the final effort, the announcer threw down the script and said, "There you are, dumb peasants."

My boss jumped on him hard. "Listen, Buster," he said.

"Those dumb peasants, as you call them, are my customers. They're important to me, a lot more important than you are."

The announcer tried to excuse himself with, "I just did it for a laugh," but his words showed how he felt about the people he was trying to sell.

Forget words that indicate lack of intelligence, such as: moron—dope—dummy—silly—asinine—cracked—ignorant—stupid.

Clear your vocabulary of such terms as: holes in head—scatterbrain—lame brain—screw loose—mentally retarded—lost his marbles.

Any such depreciation can't help you move up. When you indicate that another is dumb, you are really saying, "I'm the smart one."

Never tell another—

"You don't understand."

Doesn't that indicate he is too stupid to understand? Say instead—

"Am I making myself clear?"

Credit everybody with brains and good common sense. The others feel they deserve that rating.

5. Don't Downgrade the Jobs or the Work of Others

Every worker thinks his job is important; he feels that he is important, too. Tell a man that his job is repetitive (the experts' way of saying that he does the same thing over and over, and that his job doesn't call for much mental effort), and why should he like it? He can cite cases that show he has to use his judgment many times each day. To management his work may be repetitive, but to him his work helps keep the company going. Forget such words as "just" or "only" when you refer to jobs. How would you feel if anyone said about you—

He's just a clerk
He's only an accountant

He's one of the bookkeepers
He's got a small job in advertising.

Not quite a nobody, is it? But close. Use terms that indicate more importance. How about—

"He handles our accounts receivable"
"He helps keep us solvent"
"He is in charge of our cooperative advertising."

6. Watch Status Inference

The sociologists have invented a vocabulary to describe people that are socially, financially, or mentally inferior to us. The use of such terms indicates you feel you are superior to such people. I advise you to forget—

the have-nots
the underprivileged
the ethnics
the hard core
the deprived
the bewhiskered
the unwashed
the dropouts

On hearing such terms, the listener might wonder, "How does this guy classify me?" The terms indicate that you are of a higher order, that others rate far below you on the social scale. They also indicate that you might possibly be a bit of a snob; do you like snobs?

7. Pay Attention to All

If Jack gets his picture in the newspaper because he pulled the little boy out of the ditch, mention it to him. If Hank rolls a 300 game, ask some questions about it. If Tom's daughter is pictured as the teenager of the week, congratulate Tom. Such awareness helps you get a rating as a human being, one who is alive to what's going on around him. If you let such opportunities pass, the other might think, "He's just jealous because it didn't happen to him." Notice such things and comment on them.

8. Don't Fawn on the Brass

Why become over-courteous when you speak to those above you in your company or your club? Last week an executive took me in to meet his company president. The executive "Mistered" the poor president over and over. It was "Mister Ajax" at the start or end of every sentence. I was embarrassed, and later the big man told me, "I hope you don't get the idea that I require that kind of deference from my executives."

Changing your brand of courtesy when you contact those above you tells your associates and employees how you feel about those below. Treat everybody alike and you have no such problems.

The Right Attitude Can Carry You Far

Follow the eight bits of advice given here, and what you say and how you say it will help show the attitude that others like. Show you like your job, your work, your fellow workers, your social contacts, and you will be rated high by the king-makers who can help you on your way to your TOP.

19

Keeping Your Worries from Holding You Back

Talk about them and they slow you down. Tell your worry about the ills of the day to another worrier and what happens? He brings up one of his. Now you are started, and only the limits of your imaginations will stop you. How is that kind of talk going to help you reach your TOP?

On one of my jobs I ate lunch every day with a group of associates at a reserved table in a restaurant. The group made a rule that anyone who mentioned a worry as we talked had to buy the lunch. Mighty few were ever penalized under that rule.

The man who proposed the rule asked, "What do you learn from the other fellow's worries?" George Washington put it, "Worry is the interest paid by those who borrow trouble."

A Time for Worriers

These times are boom times for worrywarts. A worrier can kid himself by thinking, "It's the intelligent who worry about such things as: inflation—gun registration—environment—civil rights—narcotics—crime on the streets—automation."

Think over your list of acquaintances. Don't you know a few you dodge because you don't want to listen to them talk about their worries? You may feel exactly as the worrier does about the subject, but you try to avoid him. In addition to the "thinker" excuse, the worrier may add, "I know I worry a lot, but somebody must." Perhaps somebody should, but if you are known as one who talks about your worries, you are not going to get along too well with the people around you.

What Talk of Your Worries Does to You

Think of these liabilities the worrier brings on himself—

He endangers his health.
He undermines his confidence.
He wastes time, his own and his listeners'.
He becomes a pessimist.
Others run when they see him coming.

You can probably add to that list, but can't you move ahead faster without any of those reactions?

How to Avoid Becoming a Worrywart

If you have worries, don't let talk about them hold you back. Try these devices to cure yourself of worry.

1. Ask Yourself, "What Was I Worrying About This Time Last Month?"

OK, what were you worrying about? What happened to that worry? It passed, didn't it? It left you unharmed, in good health and able to show up for work on time. Anything you might be worrying about today can be handled in that same way. Forget the worry; go ahead as if you didn't have it. If you fail because of any of the troubles you imagined, you can say, "Well, I tried."

2. Reject All Worries You Can't Do Something About

This thought was given to me by a psychologist. His example was—if you have a knock in the engine of your car, you can handle that. Don't think about it. Go out to the service station and turn the worry over to the mechanic. Nurse a worry and it builds up.

About ten days ago a friend told me that he had a crick in his elbow; he said he thought it was a pulled muscle. Yesterday I saw him again. He hadn't seen the doctor about the elbow, but now he thought it was a touch of arthritis. If he doesn't do anything about the elbow for another ten days, I'm sure his diagnosis will be something worse. Doing something now sets you free.

3. Cover Yourself with Work

The other day I heard a man say, "I'm too busy to worry about anything." Work is a great antidote for worry. One executive who had reached retirement age and had tried doing nothing for six months told me, "I took this job down at the "Y" without pay. I was going nuts from worrying."

"What are you worrying about now?" I asked.

"Nothing, just about getting to work and back."

If you are worrying about anything, try losing yourself in work.

4. Try a Bit of Optimism

Think of the bright side. The complainer never seems to be happy or to have hope. His words indicate he sees only black days ahead. In earlier chapters I have advised, "Make a list of the good." Let's say the company has decided to start work an hour early and finish an hour early during the summer months. You don't like the idea, but instead of complaining, think of the good things about the move. An extra hour for garden work, a chance to get in nine holes, picnics, trips to the beach—go on, add to the list. You may find that you have more to like than dislike. When the plan was proposed, the management found more advantages than disadvantages. Talk about the good, the benefits, the advantages, and you'll find that you have less time for talk about your objections to the change.

Think of it this way—

"Worry is a kind of insult to the Lord. It is like throwing His promises and assurances back into His face and saying they are no good and you don't trust Him."

COVER UP YOUR WORRIES

Go along with one of my friends, who has a card with this lettering under the glass on his desk—

"Why should I worry, why should I fret?
Neither ever got me anything yet."

Never say, "I am worried about this." Such words can only lead you downhill. Why not go along with this advice from Robert Jones Burnett—

"There are two days in the week I never worry about—one is yesterday, the other is tomorrow."

Why let talk of your worries slow you down on your way to your TOP?

20

Complaints Can't Help You Advance

"Gus is always bellyaching."
What picture does that give you of Gus? Well, tell me this—

Do you think—
you would like him
like to work with him
does he sound like a companion you'd select to pal around with,
to bowl with, to play golf with?

You know the answers to those questions.
If you know one who fits that description—you don't want him
for a boss, or an officer of your club, because you don't want to listen
to him complain; management doesn't want him as a supervisor,
either.

How Complaining Holds You Back

Probably the most damaging complaints are those about your
own ability. Think of these ways your big mouth can depreciate your
competence.

Your Memory

One of my associates says, "I cannot remember names." When another, who has corrrected that fault, hears the remark, what does he think? If the speaker really wants to, he could learn to remember names without much trouble. Such a remark can tell others that the complainer would rather complain than reform.

Your Work Overload

Complain that you are always loaded with work and the listener may think you are not making the best use of your time, or are not too efficient. He can't get a picture of you as a big producer, can he? All because your big mouth has sounded off about the load of work the boss has given you.

Your Feelings

Maybe someone did slight you by not giving you credit for doing a job or not inviting you to a meeting, but when you hear an individual beef about such a slight, what do you think? That the other carries his feelings around where they can be bruised, or that he is too sensitive to be working in a tough business like the one he is in.

Your Health

You need all of your health and energy to move up to your TOP, and any remark depreciating either can be held against you. If you have allergies that affect you or a bad back that you have to take to the osteopath regularly, talk about them as little as possible. Talk about the exercises or the jogging you do every day, but talk about them only enough to give others the idea that you are trying to take good care of yourself. Too much talk may indicate to others that you are a nut on diet, special foods, or exercise. Don't urge your fellow workers to do as you do. They will avoid you if you do.

The Cooperation You Get from Others

Anything you say about the poor cooperation you get can be interpreted by others as a complaint against you. If the one who hears you gets good cooperation from those you accuse, why shouldn't he figure that the lack of rapport is perhaps your fault?

The Rejection of Your Ideas

Say, "I bring all these to the boss and that's all I hear of them." That's a subject to be talked over with the boss, not with others in the office. The others may think you offer too many screwy ideas. They may feel you are a poor salesman of your ideas. To move ahead, a man must be able to get his ideas accepted.

How to Stop Complaining

Before you complain about anything, try one of these devices:

1. Get On the Positive Side

Most projects have some advantages. Think of these and mention them. Perhaps you thought the publication the club put out was a waste of money, but why not say, "It was beautifully written" or "We need more communication."

When you talk about yourself, say—

"My memory for names is improving"
"I work better when I'm overloaded"
"My health was never better"
"I like these tough assignments."

2. Check Your Work Procedures

Let's say you made a proposal to your boss, and he turned you down. Don't beef to your wife, "I did all that work and he turned me down without giving the idea the consideration it deserved." Instead of blaming him, ask yourself, "What did I do wrong?" Ask such questions as—

Did I pick the wrong day or time of day?
Had he just heard some bad news?
Was he trying to get out a report to his boss?
Did he have a terrible cold or a hangover?
Did he ask a question I couldn't answer?

Answers to questions such as these help determine what went wrong. Don't blame it on the boss until you have checked to see if and where you were at fault.

3. Don't Assume Personal Affronts

It is easy to think that the one who turned down your request doesn't like you, but I'll say this—not many of your proposals are turned down because the man on the receiving end doesn't like you. You have to think of the listener. John McCarthy, a sales consultant, puts it, "Maybe if you had the decision-maker's problems, you'd be an SOB too."

Thinking about why you did not get approval will usually leave you with the conclusion that there were other considerations that had nothing to do with his like or dislike of you. Complain to others about the treatment you get and you may be tagged a crybaby.

When to Complain and How to Complain

This advice on complaining thus far applies to the petty annoyances that most of those around you never notice. However, there are times when we should complain.

Let's assume that an executive is passed over for promotion. He was the next in line and felt the promotion should have gone to him. This is a situation in which he feels he should complain, even though he knows that no complaint of his can change the decision. He approaches his boss with some questions, such as—

"Was I considered for the promotion?"
"What factors worked against me?"

With such questions answered, he can ask other questions that indicate how he stands with the management. He can decide whether he should stay with the company and work for the new appointee, or whether he should look elsewhere. If he handles the interview with questions he will do better than if he complains about the bad deal he got, about management failing to take into account the years of loyal service to the company. Make this your rule on complaints you think justified.

1. Complain only about important things, and
2. Handle your complaints with questions that indicate you may have some faults that you don't know about.

Think of Complaints as Dust and Soot

Dr. William Osler gave this advice:

"Learn to accept in silence the minor aggravations, cultivate the gift of taciturnity and consume your own smoke, with an extra draught of hard work, so that those about you may not be annoyed with the dust and soot of your complaints."

"Dust and soot"—that's about how others react to any complaint.

Somewhere I read this quote—

"Nothing is easier than fault finding. No talent, no brains, no character are required to set up in the grumbling business."

If you are in that business, get out. Replace the effort it requires with work on a skill that shows talent, brains, and character. All three will help you move faster toward your TOP.

21

You'll Always Win If You Let Others Do the Arguing

Stay out of such conversations as—

No, I don't.
Yes, you do.
No, I don't.

Dodge such exchanges, and you'll win friends and promotions.

It may be proper to argue about voters turning down school levies, but there is no excuse for arguing about the trivia that causes the hottest arguments. Read the letters to the sports editors and you hear of men arguing about such earthshaking subjects as—who played first base for Cleveland in 1937?

Such arguments waste time and energy. You may have kindred souls at your job who love to argue about such trifles, but while they are arguing other workers are working at improving skills that will help them move up. Who wins in that competition?

Love to Argue and You Face These Problems

Maybe you are one who loves to argue about anything. You leap to it with glee and gusto. If so, think of these reactions of others to the one who argues.

Others Avoid You

Most of us don't want to agree with the arguer because that encourages him to elaborate. We don't want to differ because that might bring on a tirade that reflects on our intelligence, ancestry, or what not. You have heard of the salesman who won the argument but lost the sale. Remember that most people don't like their beliefs questioned. They long for peace and quiet, and an argument can disturb that.

They Think You're Vain

Because you try to win every argument, others think you are vain. So often the arguers are not looking for the truth. They are trying to demonstrate that they are right. Bishop Fulton J. Sheen put it this way: "What is important to them is not the truth of things, but their being right."

They Distrust You

I went into the service department of a chain store to get a part I needed for an appliance. The men behind the counter were in an argument about who was to blame for a mistake that had been made the day before. One man took my order and got the part for me, but he continued to argue while he waited on me. I opened the package and checked the part. "What's the matter, Mister?" the man asked.

"I'm just checking to see if this is the part I need," I said. "I don't want to take it home and then have to make another trip out here."

The argument had shaken my confidence in the ability of the arguer to get me the right part.

Your Bosses Don't Like Arguers

You can see this in department meetings. Some employees can discuss a subject before the group, while others can't get started before the boss shuts them up. His policy may be, "Everybody has a voice in my meetings," but why does he stop some of the men before they get started? Check this at your next meeting. Isn't it because the ones he gives the opportunity to speak are offering ideas, not trying to start a rhubarb?

The president of a company warned me about one of his assistants, "Don't get into an argument with this man."

"About what?" I asked.

"About anything. This guy is a born arguer. If he could break that habit, we could make something out of him."

When the one who has the reputation for arguing is up for promotion in his company or his club, someone up above can say, "Not that guy; we don't need an arguer for that job."

How to Break the Habit of Arguing

You may say, "I don't want to stop. I love it." But don't you love success more? Then try these devices.

1. Listen

This knack can help cure many speaking faults. Don't be too eager to blast out at what the other says. Hear him out. Remember the old adage, "You never learn anything while yakking."

2. Ask Questions

Think of Kipling's six honest serving men: who—where—what—why—when—how. Perhaps you didn't understand what the other meant by his first remark. His answers to your questions help you determine if you are talking about the same thing. Use questions like—

Where did you hear that?
Do you feel your source is reliable?

Have you looked it up in the record book?
Why would they want that?

Keep any belligerence out of your voice. Ask the questions and pause as though you expect an answer.

3. State Your Beliefs with Reason

Think of this advice from Benjamin Franklin—
"The way to convince another is to state your case moderately and accurately. Then scratch your head and/or shake it a little and say that is the way it seems to you but that, of course, you may be mistaken. This causes your listener to receive what you have to say and, like as not, turn about and try to convince you, since you are in doubt, that you are right."
You don't lose friends when you admit—

you may have something in that idea
    or
that might work.

Use that type of comment and add—"tell me more."

4. Let the Others Win at Times

In assigning me to work with a group, one of my bosses said, "Let them win an argument now and then." I had no idea I needed such advice. When I questioned him about it, he added, "You have had more experience than the others and you might be inclined to dominate them." Think of this idea—if possible, let the other do the job his way; listen to his suggestion. You know how you dislike a supervisor who is always ordering, "Do it this way." Use such comments as—

"I never heard it explained that way."
"That's a good idea."

5. Avoid Taboo Subjects

Politics, religion, and race top the taboos. If you have strong opinions on any of them and voice those opinions to others who don't have similar views, you start arguments. Logic and reason don't count in such discussions; emotion takes over. State your honest views on such subjects and you become a leftist, a revolutionary, a racist, a bigot—any name the other thinks will cut you down to size. He is not trying to argue with you or discuss his ideas—he is trying to discredit you and your ideas.

6. Show Respect for His Ideas

In a day's time you may hear a lot of far-out ideas. Yesterday I read about one sportswriter walking out of a restaurant and leaving the hot dog he had ordered when another writer put ketchup on his frankfurter. One guy liked ketchup on his hot dog, while another was outraged. That's how we are—different. There was little sense in making a court case out of such a minor difference of opinion. Respect the other fellow's ideas. Let him expound them. Ask him questions about them. He feels they are good; let him feel that way. Maybe you can't understand why an intelligent individual would differ from you on a proposal, but remember, not too many people like ketchup on hot dogs; some don't like hot dogs, and some don't like ketchup.

None of us likes to hear—

"That's so wrong I'm surprised you fell for it."
"Somebody did a snow job on you."
"Let me put you straight."

Such statements indicate that the speaker is looking for a brawl.

7. Forget "Want to Bet"

The other day I commented on the death of a young man. I said, "And he was only forty-seven." My luncheon companion said, "He was only forty-two." I said, "I thought I read forty-seven." He said, "Would you like to bet five dollars on that?"

There was no call for a bet; the issue wasn't that important to him or to me. I had never bet a nickel with the man before, so he had no reason to think I would bet. I told him I never bet on issues like that, but the exchange told me something about the man. It made me think of a statement by Samuel Butler—"Fools for arguments use wagers."

Most people don't like to bet on things that are of no concern to them. You can't win a popularity contest by asking, "Want to bet?" or advising, "Put your money where your mouth is." The listener is likely to rate the one pining for a bet as a person looking for an argument.

8. Reject Argument-Starting Words

Your experience shows you that certain words and phrases start arguments in the group in which you work and play. Stop using phrases such as—

Is that so—
That's ridiculous—
You and who else—
That's a lot of hogwash—
Where did you get that screwy idea?

Any such expression asks for argument. Cut such expressions from your vocabulary. You'll cut down the time you spend arguing if you do.

How to Win Every Argument

You have heard the statement, "You can't win them all." One way you can win every argument is to follow Dale Carnegie's advice—

"The way to get the best of an argument is to avoid it."

You can't convince by argument. Remember the poem you learned years ago—

"He that agrees against his will
Is of the same opinion still."

Mr. Dooley, Finley Peter Dunn's character, said there were three ways out of an argument—"running, fighting, or cussing."
How can any of these speed your progress toward your TOP?

22

Courtesy Sets You Apart

Score big by being courteous. You'll stand out because too few of us remember.

Last night was trick-or-treat night in my town. Once I opened the front door and dropped candy bars into six bags held for me by small-fry goblins and ghosts. As the group turned to run away, I asked, "Which one of you guys said thanks?"

All of the kids turned and shouted, "Thanks."

Most of us are like that. We know we should be courteous, but we have to be reminded. How long has it been since you said—

"Please" or "Thank you?"

How You Lose by Forgetting Courtesy

Think of the ways you lose when you forget courtesy.

You Embarrass Others

This applies to associates to whom you are always courteous. They can't bear to see others take a beating. Maybe you get a kick out of ordering a waiter around, but others with you object and they rate you as one who enjoys jumping on little people.

You Are Rated as Being Rude

You may ask, "What difference does that make?" Think of an associate that you consider rude to others. How do you rate him? Crude—unlearned—boorish—backward—ignorant—foolish? Isn't it possible that those above rate you in one of those ways?

Employees Don't Cooperate

Workers cooperate better with people they like. You may think, "They have to cooperate with me, or else." But they are not compelled to like it, or to go all out. They slow down, take their time. They don't make decisions because they don't want to get chewed out. They run to the shop steward. One supervisor told me that he had a visit from the union steward with the complaint that the supervisor had spoken in a growl to a worker that morning. Sounds ridiculous, but the worker thought he didn't have to take such treatment from anybody.

They Distrust You

If you're rude to those below you and most courteous to those above, both sides wonder about you. What are you—a gentlemen or a boor, a Dr. Jekyll or Mr. Whats-his name? I went to a company cafeteria with a company executive and as we entered the room, I stopped at the end of the line. "No, no, we can go up to the front," he said, and led me past those waiting in line. As we reached the middle of the line, we ran into the top executive of the company and stopped to talk to him. We then moved with him up to the food servers. Later I said to my guide, "I thought you said we could go up to the head of the line."

"We could have, but I wanted you to meet the big boss," he said.

He knew we should have stopped at the rear of the line, but he was one who would cut in on the troops—but not on the captain.

"Do you always go to the head of the line?" I continued.

"Sure, my time's worth more than theirs, isn't it?" On that

basis, the boss's time was worth more than his, but the boss waited in line.

Others Rate You Negatively

Observers may feel your rudeness is a cover-up for some weakness and wonder what that weakness is. They feel your bluster may be put on because you are trying to appear more important than you are. Don't you rate the rude as ignorant? If not, then how do you rate them? You don't give them a plus rating, do you? Instead of helping you, a tough attitude tends to degrade you.

WHY RUIN YOUR DAY?

The other day I heard a supervisor bawl out an employee. He yelled and screamed and used language that made the employee feel like a worm. Later he apologized to me for the outburst. "I had to tell him off," he explained, "he was getting out of hand."

"How do you feel about it?" I asked.

"I'm completely worn out. I won't be worth anything the rest of the day."

I am sure you have had this feeling. Think of the times you made an unkind remark. It bothered you, didn't it? As you studied what brought on the remark, you wondered why you made it. The boss mentioned above knew that the employee should have been reprimanded, but he also knew that it shouldn't have been done in front of an audience. By handling it in that manner he got a bad mark from everybody.

How to Be More Courteous

Often, when I witness a rude act or hear a discourteous remark, I am almost certain that the offender doesn't know that he is being rude. Every day you see others make mistakes that you are sure can't be intentional. Think of these devices:

1. Use "Please" and "Thanks"

Use "please" and "thanks" more than you now do. Sunday I told the little girl down the street that her dress was pretty. She said,

"Thank you." Too many of us think that such courtesy shows weakness. Forget that idea. Everybody likes it.

2. Shun Depreciating Names

Waitresses in most restaurants have tags with their names on them. Look at the tags, then call the girl "Mildred;" that's better than, "Hey, you—." Perhaps it will get you better service, but the better service is not the objective; you're practicing being polite. Forget such nicknames for friends or associates as: Shorty—Slim— Crip—Gimpy—Fatso—Tubby. If "Tubby" is starving himself on 1200 calories per day, you don't make friends with him by using that term.

Use the other's professional name. One woman who heard her M.D. husband called by his first name said, "Maybe you don't think he is much of a doctor, but he worked for fifteen years to get that designation."

AVOID ANY BELITTLING

Watch disparaging questions like—

How can you be so stupid?
Chicken, are you?

The other day I heard a fellow tell another,

"You're cheap."

Could you tell a friend he was cheap?
You hear others described as—

stingy—dishonest—inept—dumb—a fumbler—failure—fanatic— creep—no-account.

Go on, add to the list. Forget such names or terms for anybody. The use of such terms downrates you with your listener.

3. Forget Telling Others Off

Some individuals take great pride in their ability to cut others down to size. This may give the cutters a sense of superiority, but it makes no friends with the victim or those who hear it. This story illustrates how the other feels:

I recommended a young man for a job and made a date for him to be interviewed by his prospective boss. While he was waiting in the outer office, the big man bounced out of his office and bawled out a sales representative of a supplier with such vehemence that my friend never stayed for the interview. "Didn't you want the job?" I asked.

"Yes, I did want it. It sounded as if it was made to order for me. But I wouldn't work for that so and so for any amount of money."

"Didn't you talk to him at all?" I asked.

"No, he told me what it would be like working for him."

You may feel fine when you can say—

I told him off
I put him in his place
I showed him who was boss around here.

If you commit such a sin, don't tell anybody about it, and don't let anybody hear you. Nobody looks up to the one who jumps on people who can't fight back.

4. Don't Interrupt

You know it is rude to interrupt another when he is speaking. When your teen-age son tries to tell about an incident at school, don't break in with, "They allow you to do that at school?" Let him talk; you listen. When you interrupt, he tells his pal down the street, "My old man knows everything." Let others talk, you listen, and you'll get a better rating by those who have to speak to you.

5. Avoid Stories That Make Fun of Ethnics

Don't tell stories about ethnic characters that might offend. Follow these two rules:

(a) Don't tell stories that insult minorities, and
(b) Don't tell stories that insult your own kind of ethnic. It is no excuse to say, "I can tell such stories about my people, they'll

take it from one of their own." Don't be too sure. Why make fun of your own? You should be on their side.

6. Practice at Home

Walter A. Heiby says, "Virtually all insulting things that are said are said to loved ones—wives, husbands, children—to those who will forgive, even when treated meanly." Isn't this a shame? We beat up the people who love us enough to forgive us. Try to be more courteous to your father, mother, wife, children, and the other relatives you talk with every day. Use your home as a place to practice being kind and considerate. The practice will carry over into your business and social contacts.

7. Try to Be More Courteous to Everyone

You leave your car in a parking place. You and a friend get out of the car. An attendant gets into the car to park it and as you walk away, you yell at the attendant, "Hey, boy, run up those windows." What should you have said?

My thought—leave out the "boy." (Perhaps that attendant is forty years of age.) Then, how about "please?"

If you use that parking lot often, call that attendant by name. Instead of, "Hey, boy—" make it, "Hey, Leo—." When you take your car to the manufacturer's service station, ask the man his name, and call him by his first name. This is a skill that leaders develop. They get the cooperation of little people, not only because they are big shots, but because they treat everybody as equals.

Courtesy will help you get along with everybody. Where others forget the nice thing to do, you remember it, and you help smooth your path toward your TOP.

23

How to Harness Your Criticism

Hold it.

Don't let it be said of you—"That guy criticizes everything."

Whenever you find yourself about to lambast a group, an idea, or a plan, hold it. Get tagged as a "constant criticizer" and you will hold yourself back from promotion. Nobody wants the constant critic in a position of authority. The workers don't, and the executives don't, either.

How Can You Gain by Constant Criticism?

Men who are infected with this virus feel it shows they are superior in some way. One told me,

"I'm the only one with courage enough to say what I think."

Forget any such guff. Chronic criticism is a habit that may boost your ego, but it can keep you out of the job ahead.

How Many Critics Are Your Friends?

If another criticizes you, how do you feel about him?

If you hear him criticizing another, what's your opinion of him?

If he criticizes his company or the management, he turns you off, doesn't he?

What the Urge to Criticize Does to You

It doesn't make friends, that's for sure. Assume you are one of these chronic critics. Think of the ways your repeated criticisms can harm your public relations.

You Discourage Others

Let's say you think one of the company's new products is a mistake. You say, "It won't sell; the public will make a turkey out of it fast." The ones who hear you wonder if what you say is true. They will worry about what you said, and none of them will speak as enthusiastically about the new product as they normally would. The attitude inspired by your criticism may be a factor in the failure you predicted.

Your Opinion Isn't Asked

If your social group plans a picnic or a bus trip to Cleveland to a ball game, the critic's opinion won't be asked. The organizers know in advance that you will have plenty against it. This attitude at the office, at home, or at the club may leave you out of projects in which you'd like to take part.

Your Motives Are Questioned

Others wonder why you are so quick to criticize the ideas or work of anybody. What is your real motive? Are you afraid someone will show himself to be smarter than you? Are you jealous, envious? Do you get a kick out of being against? When another asks you for an opinion of his idea or plan, he wants approval. Blast out at his brainchild and even though you offer a number of logical arguments against it, the idea man wonders if you are sorry you didn't think of the idea before he did.

Others Connect You With Your Bad Habit

I told an executive that I had met another man from his company, and he asked, "What was wrong the day you met him?" I thought back, and the man I met had mentioned a number of his pet peeves. You know how you are ready to run when one of these self-appointed critics start. If he is in your share-the-ride club, wouldn't you like to make other arrangements? If everybody runs from you, how can you get ahead?

How to Stop Criticizing

1. Watch Your First Words

Your first thought may be, "That's a crazy idea." OK, make that, "That's an idea." When your wife brings home the new hat and tries it on to get your opinion, say, "It does something for you." It does, doesn't it? When the teenager explains the project he is working on at school, ask, "Wait a minute, explain that a bit slower, will you please?" Follow those first words with some questions that indicate the other has a right to his say and you'll get further away from indicating that your ideas are the only good ones.

2. Declare a Moratorium

The buzz sessions put on by discussion leaders work on the idea that a participant can make any suggestion, no matter how far-out, and no one can criticize it. If you have attended one of these sessions, you no doubt have been surprised at the number of ideas the confreres submit. Why? Because they know it will not be criticized. With this assurance, they stick out their necks. I had one boss who had a card under the glass on his deak that read—"LET'S HAVE A MORATORIUM ON CRITICISM." You seldom influence another's thinking by criticism. Why not a moratorium?

3. Forget the Buffer Expressions

How do you feel when another starts a comment on something you did with—

"I don't like to tell you this—"
"I'm telling you this for your own good—"

You don't like them, do you? Maybe the speaker means well, and his advice may be appropriate, but he doesn't improve his image with you by offering his criticism. Forget such buffer expressions. They don't ease the pain. How can the one criticized think that your criticism is for his own good?

4. Say Something Good

This advice will eliminate all bad feelings caused by criticism. One man in my speech clinic said, "If you can't say anything good, keep your big mouth shut." There is little sense in much of the criticism you hear. I read in a newspaper account that a friend had gone off to a meeting. The next time I saw him on the street I asked, "How was the meeting?"

'They didn't seem too well-organized," he said.

We talked awhile and he mentioned a talk he heard. "It was great, Ed," he said, "you would have loved it."

I wondered why he hadn't mentioned that talk first. He would have left a better impression, of himself and the meeting. If there was nothing good about the meeting, he might have said, "They had a great entertainment program."

5. Forget That Adjective "Constructive"

One man in my clinic said, "I don't hesitate to criticize, but it is all constructive." Another says, "I don't mind criticism if it is constructive." Constructive to whom? Any criticism is seldom constructive to the one criticized. The critic may feel that he is dealing out constructive, helpful suggestions, but the one on the receiving end seldom feels that way.

6. Don't Be Fooled By—"I Can Take It"

Few of us can. The speaker who asks for criticism with a remark like that thinks he means what he says, but if you tear into his idea, he won't like it. He will blame you for criticizing an idea that he thinks is good.

7. Criticize in Private

This is one of the rules of good management. There have been times when you have heard a supervisor criticize a worker in front of a whole department. Do you remember which you felt sorrier for—the critic or the victim? Both needed sympathy. This week, one of the sports magazines carried an article about a football coach. One of the reasons the players didn't like the coach was that the coach criticized players in front of the whole squad. One player said, "If he thinks he has to chew a guy out, he should take him inside his office and close the door." The closed door helps when a boss is bawling out one of his employees. He has the right to criticize—but beware of any criticism that you don't get paid for.

8. Let the Criticized Help

Trainers have a plan that takes most of the sting out of criticism. Assume the worker is being taught a task and makes certain mistakes. In correcting him, the trainer follows these steps:

First, he compliments the worker on something he did well. For instance—

"You have those first two movements exactly right—"

Second, he asks questions to get the worker to tell what he didn't do right on the movements that followed.

The trainer doesn't tell the worker; the worker will do the telling if the trainer asks the right questions.

Third, he agrees that the worker knows what he did wrong. He drills him on the right way. He gets agreement that the worker knows the correct way.

Fourth, he encourages the worker on his progress.

I give this procedure in detail because it indicates how important it is for the one criticized to understand the mistake, and to work out his own way to correct it in the future. Shouting and name calling can do little more than antagonize the worker.

CRITICS DON'T RATE TOO HIGH

The wife of a friend of mine, after listening to a critic on TV lambast a movie, said, "That nut would be tough to live with." Critics are hard to live with. If you have a wife who disapproves of any of your habits or a boss who loves to criticize, you understand why Sacha Guitry put it—

"The world is filled with statues of writers, poets and musicians. Have you ever seen a statue of a critic?"

If possible, stay away from criticizing anything. Your criticism, no matter how well-intentioned, won't help you reach your TOP.

24

Letting Others Play the Clown

"He's always good for a laugh."

You know men who fit that description. Don't try to imitate them. Here is why—

I had a young man in one of my sessions who had the knack of getting laughs with his comments and the questions he asked. After the session I told him, "You have an active sense of humor."

"I know it," he answered, "but the boss tells me I'd better cool it."

The boss has a point. The one who is always ready with the wisecrack is popular, his cracks brighten the day's work, but he mav be thought too frivolous to be put in a leader's position.

Where Do Laughs Get You?

An imitation of Fatso, the Grand PooBah of the Lodge, going through his official ceremonies may be a classic, but how will it help the mimic move up to a higher office? Others may think those ceremonies beautiful. They feel "Fatso" does them with the dignity

160

LETTING OTHERS PLAY THE CLOWN

they deserve. Of course some members laugh at the joker's comedy, but they rate him lower than the member with no such flair. Associates may tell him, "You should be on TV."

What do the ones who consider him for higher office remember? Isn't it—what a great entertainer he is? And entertainers aren't what they want for those higher offices.

Check This at Your Club or Lodge

Isn't the jester's job: membership committee—caller at bingo—master of ceremonies at the social affairs? On such jobs those men are great. They get lots of compliments and sincere applause, but the same people who laugh and applaud wonder about the joker's ability as a leader. The laugh-maker seldom gets into the line that leads to his election as the Grand PooBah.

How About the Clowns at the Office?

It is much the same at the shop—the one who is ready with the laugh line is not on what you would call a very important job. He is popular; everybody is his friend. The top executives call him by his first name. They invite him on their fishing and hunting trips; he sits in on their poker games. Although his job doesn't rate with theirs, he has bets with them on sporting events, but he isn't holding down a very important job. You'd think with such friendships with the bosses he would move up fast, but he doesn't move up even as fast as you think his ability warrants. Those big shots, his buddies who do the promoting, think of him as a clown. They love him, his disposition, his humor, and his ability to get a laugh out of anything. Perhaps they wish they could promote him, but they are afraid to take a chance.

Making a Living Is a Serious Business

Most executives feel this way. The laughs are good for morale, yes—but they don't help much in running a department, a business, a lodge, or a club. Top men understand this and they feel that a serious person will do better running a serious job.

Comedy Calls for Work

I worked with a minor executive who was a master of coming up with the humorous crack that broke up meetings and arguments. Associates asked, "Where does he get these witty remarks?" I once asked him how much time he estimated he put in on developing his skill. "About fifteen minutes each day," he said.

Executives who may think of promoting the comedian have a suspicion that he puts a lot of time in developing his skill. They may say—

At the job—"If he put in that much time developing his skill as a manager, he would be more help to us."

At the club—"If he put in that much time getting us new members, he would help us more."

There is good common sense in both thoughts.

Forget the Horseplay

I heard the chairman of a meeting break up a big laugh with these words: "Let's get on with the work, first." This is the idea the leaders of your business, club, or social group try to follow. "Business comes first."

One misfortune that TV has brought us is that it has inspired too many people to think they should try to be funny. Forget any such urge. You'll get ahead faster as a serious worker.

Let the other fellow try for the laughs. You try for talk that makes sense. Being an artist with the wisecrack can keep you from moving to your TOP.

25

Keeping Mistakes in English from Holding You Down

Can others say of you, "He murders the King's English?"
If they can, you are handicapping yourself needlessly. Let's say a new employee at the job asks this question—

"Ain't we got no form for this?"

You've got him pegged, haven't you? You feel he has a lot to learn before he can be promoted. Let's say he had asked—

"Do we have a form for this?"

Wouldn't that change your impression of him?

How Your Usage Rates You

I once asked an associate who lunched with me often what college he attended. He said, "I never went to college." His language was so free of the common mistakes that those who heard him speak assumed that he was a college graduate. This shows how correct usage helps your image. Stay away from a few common mistakes and nobody will question your potential because of the language you speak.

I have also worked with college graduates who were so careless with word usage that a listener might assume they had never seen the inside of a school.

There is no sense in making mistakes that the listener notices. Avoid about eight or ten common mistakes and no one will downrate you because of usage. Think of that—just eight or ten. I have heard men alibi with—

"You know what I mean, don't you?"

I did. I also knew that he was competent at his job and that he handled people well, but if he was interviewed by anyone above him for a job ahead, those mistakes in language would blur the impression he was trying to make.

Avoid These Seven Mistakes that Others Notice

The mistakes illustrated are the ones made most often, and they are also the ones most listeners notice. Not too many associates will notice mistakes you make with "will" and "shall," or "who" and "whom." The illustrations that follow show you how easy it is to correct the most noticable mistakes.

1. The Double Negative

If you use the double negative, most listeners will rate you as uneducated. I consider it the most glaring mistake, the one that jars listeners the most. Note how easy it is to correct these familiar ones you hear every day—

I don't have no money.
He can't have no ideas.
Nobody had no fun.
He never did nothing

You easily found the errors in all of these sentences. If this error might betray you, work to correct it.

2. The Do and Did, Don't and Doesn't Mistakes

This mistake shows up most often in the interchange of "don't" and "doesn't." Say—

"He don't have any right"

and you are wrong, because you wouldn't say—

"He do not have any right"

You'd say—

"He does not have any right."

Thus you'd be right if you said—

"He doesn't have any right."

When you are speaking of what one person did, you use "doesn't."

When you are speaking of one object, you use "doesn't."

When you are speaking of more than one, you use "don't," as in—

"They don't have any right."
You can say, "I don't," but you can't say, "Chuck don't."

Many of us get mixed up in the use of the words "do," "did," and "done." Mystery stories are called "Who done its," but most of us know that is an incorrect use of the word. The correct way is, "Who did it?"

Correct the usage in these sentences—

"Susie admits she done it"
"They would have did it if they had the chance"
"I should have did what I knew I should have done"

3. Use Know, Knew, Known Correctly

Almost as bad as the double negative is the use of "knowed."
There is no such form of the word, yet yesterday on the TV I heard
a man say, "I knowed they couldn't win." Mighty few of us would
make that mistake, but you do hear it, and when you hear it, what
is your opinion of the user?

4. We Misuse "Gone" and "Went"

Somehow our people seem to prefer that word, "went." You
hear such lines as—

"I wish I had went."
"If we had known there would be trouble we wouldn't have
went."

Such usage shocks listeners. The correct usage is—

"I wish I had gone."
"—we wouldn't have gone."

As you check these mistakes you will find that if the verb comes
at the start of the sentence, it is safe to use "went." If it comes at
the end of the sentence, you're safer with "gone."
For instance—

We went—
They were gone.

5. Watch the Personal Pronouns.

I had a girlfriend in high school who corrected me when I said,
"Between you and I." She was doing me a favor, but I didn't recognize it as such. (Wonder why I lost track of her?) This is a quite
common type of mistake, even by the professionals who speak on
the air. One will come up with something like, "Both of we announcers." He wouldn't say, "Both of we." No, it would be, "Both of us."
If now and then you hear a professional make such mistakes, you

can assume that they are not too easy to avoid. As you look at the sentence that follows, you probably will see the mistake—

I use better judgment than her.

If you use "I," match it with "she." If you use "me," match it with "him."

One way to check such mistakes is to complete the sentence. For instance—

You selected him rather than selecting me.
I use better judgment than she does.

Another way to dodge this mistake is to use the person's name.

You selected me rather than Charlie.
I use better judgment than Annie.

A few Sundays ago, the golf professional giving the instruction said on the TV broadcast, "It's been a bad day for he and Charlie."
That doesn't sound right, does it?
"For Charlie and him" would have seemed right.
"For Charlie and Tom" would have caused no question.
Use names instead of the personal pronouns and you will be correct every time.
Many listeners will not recognize this mistake, but some will, and those who do may rate you as one of the bruisers of the langauge.

6. Straighten Out "Was" and "Were"

Say—

"I was there." That sounds right and is right.
"You was there." Doesn't sound right, and isn't.

It should be—

"You were there"

Tom was there, Pete was there, but Tom and Pete *were* there.

7. Get Out of the "Dem" and "Dose" Class

When I mention "dem" and "dose," you think of a tough, rough type of individual. If you have any of these rough edges in your speech, try to correct them. One man told me, "I talk tough because my mother brought me up to be a sissy." As I studied him I felt that his tough talk hadn't changed him much. It didn't sound natural. He still seemed a sissy who tried to talk tough. Think of the image you want to leave with those who work or play with you. It is not that of a tough guy, is it?

ASK YOUR WIFE

I suggest this because the girls usually paid better attention in school. Ask her, "Which is my most noticeable mistake?" Don't resent her telling you; thank her for her help and start working on the fault she mentions.

If you speak so well that nobody around you notices your mistakes, your usage of the language won't interfere with your progress toward your TOP.

NOTE:

If you find you are making many of these mistakes in usage, I suggest you get a book on correct usage. Such a book will list more mistakes than I cover in this chapter. Correct the ones I mention first, then go on to others that you want to eliminate. You'll find this work interesting. You'll see rapid improvement. You'll see mistakes that others make that you might not have noticed before, but don't mention the mistakes to those who make them. Your most important job is working on your own improvement. If others ask your advice, give it, but don't initiate the advice.

26

Showing Your Good Taste by Avoiding Vulgar Language

Your TOP is not the gutter.

Then how can the use of gutter language help move you toward the bigger job, or the higher office in your lodge or club? Captains, Kings, and PooBahs rate the use of such language as a fault.

My Favorite "Damn" Adjective

A man in my speech clinic said, "Why, "damn" is my favorite damn adjective." It seems to be a favorite with many, but it is not the best adjective to express any meaning.

A friend telling me about changing a tire said, "All went well until this damn nut stuck." Think of the adjectives he could have used: stubborn—reluctant—contrary—balky—frozen—obstinate.

Maybe you say "damn" is better than any of the substitutes listed, but the choices demonstrate how your language allows you to use a much more expressive word than "damn."

What to Do about "Hell"

You may like the expression—

"I didn't know what the hell he meant."

You mean—

"I am confused."

Isn't there a better way to say that you were confused? You might have used: perplexed—puzzled—uncertain—bewildered—in a quandary. All are better than "what the hell." All give a different impression of the user.

Dodge the Four-Letter Favorites

The movies and stage plays today are filled with four-letter words that once would have shocked us. Last week in a review of a play the critic said, "Once these words shocked us; now they just bore us." Most critics praised the movie "LOVE STORY," but expressed regret that the author had put the four-letter vulgarities into the mouth of his beautiful heroine. The excuse of authors for using such words is, "This is the way people talk." I'll not argue about that, but my advice to the young man or woman who wants to advance is to invoke your own fifth amendment against such words. They tend to incriminate and degrade you. You may get a kick out of the shock they give, but you'll never move up in your club or your business on the strength of a foul mouth. The Puritans, the prudes, and the Comstocks are all around you. Nobody regards a filthy mouth as an asset of a leader.

I worked with one speaker in a series of meetings. He went further than "damn," he made it "God damn." When I suggested he cut the references to the Lord, he said, "These guys don't object to it."

"Maybe God would," I offered.

"I don't believe in God," he answered.

That incident indicates how silly it is to use any profanity.

Forget Your Dirty Stories

You may say, "Oh, no, I love them."

OK, love them, but don't get a reputation as a teller of dirty stories. How can such a reputation build you up as a solid citizen?

An associate told me he didn't think much of a representative of a supplier. I asked why. "He's always telling dirty jokes," he said. I said that I had never heard the man tell such a joke.

"How about the one he told at Tom Hansen's party?" the man asked.

I had forgotten the story, but that one dirty joke had undermined my associate's confidence in the supplier.

Consider Your Self-Respect

Men who arrange for speakers for clubs have written me, "There will be no ladies present, so you can tell any stories you want to tell." I have always wanted to answer, "I don't tell that kind of story because I'll be there." Somewhere I read a quote that went, "Self-respect is at the bottom of all good manners." You respect yourself, don't you? OK, why not respect the other fellow and show your respect for him.

How Dirty Words Smear an Executive

I once asked my boss when he was scheduled to speak to a group of young men, "Cut your cussing when you talk to these men, will you, please?"

He asked why.

"You are on the program to show these boys what our top executive looks like. If they hear you swear, they might think they have to swear as proficiently as you do to get ahead."

"I never thought of that angle," he admitted.

He made his talk without the "damns" and "hells" and his other choice four letter words.

After the question and answer period he told me, "I believe it went over better because it was cleaned up."

It did go over better. The young men thought of him as a gentlemen, not a crude roughneck.

174

Another difficulty of such a habit of the boss is that the employees have to sit and take it. One manager told me, "They can like it or not, I don't care." But it pays to care. The employees can think more highly of a boss who doesn't feel he needs the support of shocking vulgarities to strengthen his points.

Why Some Executives Use Vulgar Expressions

Men in my speech clinic gave two reasons why some business executives used such words. First, a poor vocabulary; second, the desire to be a "he" man.

A Poor Vocabulary

The speaker feels that his vulgar words add strength to his statements. I don't agree with this. The words I suggested as substitutes for the "damn" to describe the frozen nut were words that most of us know.

By using any one of the substitutes—"frozen" "obstinate"— "stubborn"—you get away from the accusation that you didn't know the words to properly express the idea—and you express it better.

The Desire to Be a "He" Man

It may be that when you tried to analyze why an associate practiced "foul mouth," you felt he was trying to build an image as a tough hombre. I once heard a beautiful young lady rattle off a selection of vulgar epithets, and my thought was that she was trying to attract attention. She looked to be too nice a girl. The vulgar words may make you appear tougher than you are, but they won't help you get promoted to the job ahead.

How to Banish the Vulgar

It is not too difficult to cut the rough edges from your talk. Try these two devices:

1. Make a List of the Words You Want to Eliminate

Start with "damn" and "hell," then add the other ones you use but consider questionable. List the names you use for men—the ones that cast reflections on their legitimacy, parentage, intelligence; the names you use for women—"dames," "broads," and "babes" may not seem vulgar, but may offend. If you use harsher words for women, list them. Now check through the body parts and functions, the sex words. Add any others that these suggestions miss. Add such words as: crap—john—nuts. Now you have a list—try to stop saying those words. You'll find it is not as difficult to stop as you might imagine. You may feel a bit self-conscious at first, but stick to the idea.

2. Find Other Words to Substitute

I demonstrated the substitution principle in the examples I gave for "damn." There were no involved words among those substitutes; you knew every one of them. It won't be too difficult to find a clean word for the vulgar one you are trying to eliminate. Many times you may feel that the vulgarity expresses the idea better than your refined substitute, but remember the old saying, "A rose by any other name—." Bruce Barton said, "Every time you open your mouth, you show the listener your mind." How can the dirty word suggest a clean mind?

Start This Easy Plan Today

Don't put off any longer—
Cut the "damns" and "hells."
Cut any four letter obscenities, or foul insulting names.
Who wants a foul mouth as the head of his company?
Or the head of his club or lodge?

Show your good taste by speaking as a gentlemen or lady should. What's the sense of building an impression that will slow you on your way to your TOP?

27

How to Improve Your Listening to Move Up Faster

Think of how you feel about the people who listen to you. They're the best, the greatest, the most competent, right?

If you become expert at listening, others will feel that way about you. I asked a neighbor about a tough supervisor he had been assigned to. "He's my friend," the man said, "he listens to me." The boss was tough, but he buffered that toughness by listening.

Another man told me, "My boss is a great manager, but he won't listen."

These are two opposites, and the second case is tragic, isn't it. If the boss won't listen, how is he going to learn anything from his help?

Check Yourself for These Faults

When you should be listening, do you—

seem impatient
show no interest
interrupt?

If you do any of these, your listening is not helping you.

What You Gain by Listening

Listening is one of the strongest tools in human relations. Think of these benefits to you:

1. The Speaker Likes You

How can he help liking you? You show that you feel he is important. So many fail to listen to him—his wife won't listen, his kids won't listen—since you listen, you stand out. He feels you are one he can trust and depend on.

2. You Learn Things

One wag puts it, "One advantage of listening is that you might learn something." A man in my speech session has said, "Everything you ever learned was learned by listening."

3. You Get to Know the Speaker

What you hear tells you much about the speaker. You never knew he was a student of Shakespeare, or came from Indiana. By listening you learn these things, and get a better appreciation of his skill, his character, his interests.

4. You Get Ideas

As you listen, something the other says sparks an idea. It may be an idea about the subject of which he speaks, or it may be an idea that has nothing to do with what he said. At times I catch myself making a note as another speaks. Last week a friend sitting next to me asked, "He didn't say anything that warranted a note, did he?" Perhaps he didn't, but he said something that started me thinking.

How to Listen

Communication is a two-way process—one talks, the other listens. We try to listen to those above us—our bosses, the officers of the lodge—but we are not so careful when we listen to those below us.

Listening is made up of three steps.

1. You hear what the other says
2. You let him know you heard
3. You show an interest.

How closely do you follow those steps?

Hearing What Was Said

Most of us hear, even though we are looking out a window or shuffling through papers on our desk. But we do a better job of listening if we look at the man, give him our full attention.

Let Him Know You Heard

A question helps tell him you have heard. Ask, "Is this what you mean?" or, "Where did you get those facts?" Such questions help assure him that you are listening, and they encourage him to tell you more.

Show an interest

A complimentary statement is good. Say, "That's a good idea," or, "I never heard of that before." A question that asks for more information can cover this step, such as, "Have you tried to estimate how much this idea will save?" Such statements or questions indicate that you are willing to hear more.

Five More Steps to Improve Your Listening

These five additional steps will make you a better listener.

Hear It All

Encourage the other to keep talking. Too often we are not told the whole story because we don't encourage the other to tell us, or we don't sympathize. When the speaker stops telling, it helps to ask, "Is that all?"

Don't Interrupt

Let the other talk on. The greatest pest is the one who breaks in to correct you. You know how you feel when you start to tell about your trip to Chicago, and your wife breaks in with, "It wasn't State Street, dear, it was LaSalle Street."

Repeat What He Said in Your Words

A salesman does this when you make an objection to something he said. This gives you a chance to say, "No, that's not what I mean." The device gets the other to restate what he said so you both know what you are talking about.

Never Say "I Know It"

A friend told me, "Every time I try to give my boss a piece of information, he stops me by saying, 'I know it.' I'm sure in many cases that he hasn't got the information, but he stops me from giving it to him." A supervisor who has this habit, even though he does know what the assistant is planning to say, cuts himself off from much information that his assistants should bring him. His group tells him nothing. They say, "That so-and-so knows everything."

Thank the Other

Even though the person has not brought you any new information, thank him for it. Assume the man advises, "Watch those speed traps down in Kentucky." Now you have driven this road in Kentucky time and again and you know about the speed traps; you also know where the special cop hides from the speeders. Well, don't spend any time informing the other of what you know. Thank him for the information and he will bring you other information.

A Good Listener Makes a Better Supervisor

I worked for a manager who sat at his desk cleaning his fingernails with a pen knife while I tried to talk to him. Every few minutes he would assure me, "Keep on, I'm listening." He probably was listening, but that manicuring job was bothering me. In my management session the men have listed fourteen things their bosses do while the men are trying to tell him something. They shuffle papers on the desk, look for a certain letter, call out a question to their secretaries—go on, mention the faults of your boss.

Here's a story about a boss who wouldn't listen.

An assistant came into his office to tell the boss that he was quitting his job. The boss, being one of the non-listeners, started to tell the assistant what he had on his mind. After a number of attempts, the assistant finally got across the idea that he was there to resign.

"Why do you want to resign a good job like this?" the boss asked.

"You're demonstrating why," the employee said.

"I'm demonstrating why—how?"

"You don't listen. I've been trying to tell you I'm quitting for twenty minutes, and you were not listening."

The assistant had a new job on which he hoped his boss would listen to him. The executive had the job of finding a new assistant. Perhaps it would have been better if the executives had worked to cure what Shakespeare called, "The disease of not listening."

Study the Art of Listening

There is a lot more to listening than can be covered in one chapter. Get a book on listening. There are a number available. If possible, take a course in listening at a local school or college. These books and courses can help you learn to listen better—and better listening will help you reach your TOP.

TIP TO LISTENERS

At the end of Chapter Eleven, I gave a bit of advice in dealing with technical jargon. It doesn't apply to the art of listening, but it helps greatly in making sure you understand. If you have listened carefully and haven't understood, ask, "Would you please explain exactly what you mean by those words?"

Count the Faults You Have Corrected

This is a good way to check your progress. Of course, you never were bothered with all of the faults listed in these last chapters. Very few of us have been, but we do see some of them as faults that afflict us. These questions will help you check on which ones you are doing something about. Remember, every little improvement helps.

What about your greetings and responses to greetings?

Do you say, "I'm wrong," more often?

Have you thrown away the words like "stupid," "dumb," "holes-in-head?"

Have you talked less about your worries and complaints?

Have you cut arguing, wanting to bet?

How many times have you said "Please" and "Thank you" today?

Have you cut your words of criticism?

Are you still trying to be the court jester?

What mistakes in language have you corrected?

Can you get through the day without a "damn" or "hell" or other vulgarity?

Are you using the devices that make you a better listener?

The answers to those questions will show how you have improved your speech since reading the preceding chapters. If you can answer "yes" to a single one of those questions, you have improved your relations with the people who live, work, and play with you, those above you and those below you.

Part V

DEVELOPING THE VOICE OF AN EXECUTIVE

"For if the trumpet gives an uncertain sound, who shall prepare for battle?"
I—Corinthians—14-8.

Doubt or indecision in the sound of your voice can hold you back. A positive voice helps you climb, as it indicates—

you know
you believe
you care
you have energy
you are enthused.

Think now of a man you consider a leader. Doesn't his voice show some or all of those qualities? A leader takes no chances of demonstrating an uncertain trumpet.

The following chapters give you ideas on developing your voice to help you as his voice helps him. They show how easy it is to make your voice a greater help in your drive toward your TOP.

28

How Speaking Up Makes Others Listen

Speak a bit louder, and the listener has a better chance to hear what you say. That bit louder makes you sound as if you—

believe what you say
mean what you say
know what you are talking about
are enthused about an idea
are interested in it
are in excellent health
have enough energy to do your job.

You can add to that list, I am sure, but look at the list again. You get all those benefits by speaking a bit louder.

The other day an associate made a remark. I asked, "What?" He asked, "Why don't you get a hearing aid?" His thinking was backwards. It is his job to speak loud enough so I can hear.

How to Check Your Volume

If you don't speak loud enough, you may not know it. The listener won't tell you. Why not check by using one or more of these devices?

Check the Questions

Do others ask what you said? Do they ask questions that indicate they haven't heard? Do they ask you to speak a bit louder? A man in my speech clinic told this story. He was a candidate for a promotion and was being interview by the top executive concerned. "Twice that man had to ask me to speak louder," he admitted. "I was excited about the interview, of course, but I wasn't speaking loud enough for him to hear without straining."

Watch the Listener's Face

His expressions may tell you that he is having difficulty hearing what you say. If he appears to be straining to hear, leans his head a bit closer, or turns his good ear, help him by turning on more volume. How many times do you adjust the volume on the radio or TV to get the volume that is right for you?

Ask the Listener

If you have doubt that the other hears, ask him if he hears. Ask, "Am I speaking loud enough?" Don't ask a question that indicates that his hearing is at fault. It is your job to make things clear to him.

Practice Getting More Volume Into Your Voice

Teachers of speaking say, "Learn to project your voice." You want your voice to carry to the ear of your listener. Here are some ways to practice.

Try Opening Your Mouth Wider

One football coach I hear interviewed on TV every week never opens his mouth enough when he explains the victory or defeat. His words coming through his teeth are not easy to hear. Next time you see one of these closed-mouth talkers on TV, note how difficult he is to understand. If you sing hymns in church, open your mouth wider when you come to, "Glory to God in the highest." Note how you find yourself singing louder. If you sing in the shower, try that idea. If you never sing, start singing. It is a good practice to add volume to your voice.

Talk Back to the Man on the Radio

I say "radio" because you can do this when you are in the car alone. Turn on a talk program and try repeating what the man says, or start arguing with him about what he says. Use a bit more volume than he uses. If the disc jockey announces that the next number will be "Four Beats and a Horse," ask, "How did you know, Charlie, that I was expecting that?"

Give Some Lessons

If your children have the habit of speaking too softly, give them some lessons in speaking up. The lessons will not be too popular with the kids, but the thought and the practice will help you put more volume into what you say.

Assume the Listener Is Slightly Deaf

One man who had the habit of not speaking loud enough told me how he broke himself of the habit. "I told myself that these listeners were slightly deaf. Then I spoke a bit louder to compensate." If your voice is difficult to hear, listeners will try to hear for a few minutes and then give up—but they won't blame themselves if they can't hear. They blame you.

It's a Noisy World

A father walks into the room where his teen-age son is doing his homework and turns off the blaring radio. "Why did you turn that off?" the boy demands.

"I wanted to talk to you," the father says.

"I could hear you with that radio going."

'But this is important," the father said.

The boy had been brought up in a world filled with noise of all kinds. He couldn't understand why quiet was needed for any conversation. The line, "A soft answer turns away wrath," was written long before bedlam took over. Today the soft answer may not be heard.

Why Commercials Take No Chances

Your favorite commentator says they will take a minute out for this important message. The message comes on, much louder than the commentator. Advertising magazines have devoted much space to criticism of this fault of TV commercials, but the commercials still come on loud. If you adjust the volume of the set so that it is about right for the commercial, when the program comes on again you have to turn up the volume. I mention this procedure to remind you that we all have volumes at which we would like the other to speak, but it will pay any of us to speak with enough volume so that the other will hear without too much effort. With most of us that means—speaking just a bit louder.

Compare Yourself With Others

You may feel that some of your friends or associates speak too loud, but these are in the minority. The greatest number don't speak loud enough. The other evening I heard a candidate for office answer a few questions for the TV newsman. A friend said, "I don't see how that joker could get elected to anything." I didn't either. The candidate showed by the volume in his voice that—

he was tired
he lacked energy
he perhaps was not in good health.

And we didn't ask, "What good qualities does he have?"
No, our question was, "Who's running against him?"
That's how it works in politics and in the life you lead in business, in social contacts, at home, and every place your voice is heard.
The voice that is difficult to hear doesn't—

show confidence
indicate enthusiasm
demonstrate leadership qu.

Who wants to follow an uncertain trumpet? So, speak up!
You'll need all of those qualities mentioned if you are to reach
your TOP.

29

How Speaking Slower Helps Listeners Understand

The other day in the polling place an official was giving instructions. I asked the lady next to me, "Do you hear him?"

"Yes, I know he is saying something, but he speaks so fast I can't understand him," she said.

She heard, but she didn't understand.

Speaking too fast is a fault of most of us. You'll hear this tonight on TV. The commentator consults an expert. You hear and understand the commentator, but while you hear the expert, he speaks too fast for you to understand.

A man in my speech clinic told me, "Our minister is the fastest talker I know; he goes so fast in his sermon that I get only about half of it."

"Have you told him he goes too fast?" I asked.

"No, and I'm not going to—we get out five minutes early because he goes so fast."

The minister worked hard on those sermons, and no doubt his parishioners needed the advice, but his speed in delivery cut the results of his hard work.

Not Sermons, Not Speeches, Just Ordinary Talk

This slow-down advice is more important when you are giving instruction, information, or orders. In so many cases it would pay us to slow down so that the other has a better opportunity to understand. I once was given the job of making a proposal to one of the top officials of my company. I figured that the executive's time was valuable and that he would want me to give him the proposal as quickly as I could. I started at high speed and had gone no further than one paragraph before the big man stopped me and said, "Now start over again and tell me that more slowly, please." Even though he was a busy man, he wanted to hear and understand.

What You Lose by Talking Too Fast

The Listener Doesn't Understand

A man rang my doorbell once, and when I answered he started a talk about why I should vote for a local school levy. He talked so fast that I didn't understand half of the points he made. I asked him if he had any idea how many votes he lost because he talked so fast. "I always talk fast like this," he said. "If you slow down more people will understand you," I told him. "I've only got a couple of minutes," he said. Which is more important—to get through the story in two minutes, or to have the listener understand?

The Listener Wonders if You Want Him to Understand

He feels you may be trying to cover up. He has been warned about the fast talkers who sell gold bricks, and when he meets a fast talker he is likely to tune out.

Your Employee Makes Mistakes

This comes because you haven't taken the time to fully explain what you want done, how you want the job done, when you want it done. Most workers will rush off to do the job. They won't ask you to clarify. That would reflect on their intelligence, right?

Your Employee Takes Unjustified Blame

When he makes mistakes he takes a blame that might not be his. A merchant in my town gave all of his employees aptitude tests. The young lady that rated highest on intelligence was one that he felt never seemed to understand. The psychologist explained that perhaps the merchant talked too fast for the young lady to follow. The store owner tried slowing up when he spoke to her, and found she was quite intelligent.

Others Can Listen Only So Fast

We all have a rate at which we listen comfortably. If you ask us to concentrate more than we find comfortable, you may lose us. Watch the next magician you see on TV. Note how slowly he talks, how slowly he does things. He wants you to hear every word, to watch every action. Compare the emcees you see on TV. You have difficulty following the fast talker. You hear the slower speaker better.

Check Yourself on Speaking Speed

One way to check is to dictate into a recorder, then listen to what you have said. Dictate the same piece slower and listen again. Try to determine a talking speed that seems best for you, your voice, your words. Then use the checks I advised for speaking too low—

watch the listener's face
check the questions he asks
ask, "Am I making myself clear?"

Six Ways to Slow Down

If you feel you are speaking too fast, think of these devices to help you make your meaning clear:

1. Use the Pause

It is your words tumbling out, one after another, that causes confusion. Say about ten words and then pause to allow the idea to sink in.

2 Ask a Question

Ask a question and pause as if you expect an answer. Watch the listener's face for the effect of the question.

3. Ask What or How

If you have given an assignment, a question about the job may get an answer that tells you whether or not the listener understands.

4. Try Repetition

If you know you are a fast talker, try repeating in different words. This gives the other two chances to understand. The listener's face will indicate how this device has cleared up the idea for him.

5. Study Your Favorite TV Voice

The chances are you like this man because you understand every word he says. Make a recording of his voice, then of your voice saying the same words. This is one advantage of radio and TV—it gives us the chance to hear scores of speakers with voices of different speeds and timing; you can study these voices and try to determine why you understand one perfectly, and do not hear or understand another.

6. Try This Slow Down Exercise

Select a twenty-word paragraph out of your evening newspaper and read it aloud at your normal rate of speed. Now read it aloud a bit slower. Then, a third time, a bit slower.

I have fast talkers in my speech clinic try this exercise. First normal speed, then slowing down a bit, then slowing down a bit more. This gives the men in the class a chance to see how a slower pace can add to the clarity of what is said.

There Is No Advantage to Talking Fast

When asked, "What do you gain by talking fast?" men in my speech session tell me it—

makes you seem smarter
indicates you know your stuff
suggests you are a fast thinker
shows you are alive, alert.

I get a number of such answers. Then I ask, "What is the objective of all talk?"

The answer comes, "To help the listener UNDERSTAND."

That's what your talk is for. So speak slowly enough for the other to understand what you said. Forget any other objective.

Help Him Hear and Understand

Your listener will like you better if you don't force him to concentrate too intently. It is no excuse to say, "I have always talked fast." Maybe you have, and perhaps at times others have failed to understand what you have said. That lack of understanding is your fault. You don't seem more competent; your fast talk impresses nobody but you. Slow down to the speed that others like. The old saying says, "Slow but sure."

Speak slowly enough for the other to hear and understand, and you'll speed your climb to your TOP.

30

How Careful Enunciation Helps Make Your Meaning Clear

Get the mush out of your mouth.
Cut slurring over sounds.
Give each syllable its chance.

I've said—

Speak up
Speak a bit slower.

Now I say—pronounce your words clearly.

All three help the other understand. They also give him a much better impression of you.

Tonight, start checking the people you listen to on TV. When the emcee introduces the beautiful girl singer, you hear his frenzied build-up of her remarkable talent, but then he pronounces her name in a way that leaves you guessing. The newsman says that some biggie was indicted, but he failed to pronounce the name of the big man so that you could hear it.

These people are professionals who make their living through speaking. If some of them can't make you understand, think of how much care you need to make others understand you.

How Poor Enunciation Handicaps You

The Listener Doesn't Hear

Think back to the last time you heard a foreigner being interviewed on TV. You tried to listen to the man, but his trouble with pronunciation bothered you. You listened for a minute or so and then tuned off. You hear the heads of state who learned their English in English schools. They don't speak our language and you have difficulty following what they say. Then you hear English sportswriters trying to describe our golf matches. They try, but they show us why our own boys are so much easier to hear and understand. The advertisers seem to think that they can use silly English butler types to sell merchandise with commercials done in mouth-full-of-mush pronounciations. Listen to a few of these characters and you will see why you need to speak as clearly as you can to help others understand.

He Downrates You

Sloppy speech tells your listener too much about you. Listen to some of the "athletes" on TV. Most of these men were taught to play some game extremely well, but they were never taught to speak to others. Thus, when they are put on the air to give the background on a sporting event, you have trouble following them. Their enunciation may be good for their part of the country, but not for the whole country.

You get this same reaction when one of these men tries to sell you a product. The advertiser may feel that because the athlete recommends his product you will buy it, but you would understand the benefits of the product better if the advertiser had hired a professional speaker.

He Feels You Are Trying to Impress

Some of the individuals you hear on TV seem to be trying to speak as the proper Bostonians or the English are supposed to. Their pronunciation and accent seem to indicate that you are inferior in some way.

I once worked with a teacher of voice who tried to change what he called the burred "R" on my word endings. Instead of "TogetheR," he had me saying, "togethAH." The "ah" ending may have been correct, but my boss told me, "Cut that "togethah" stuff, it makes you sound like a phony."

How to Check Your Enunciation

Check Other Speakers

Around the job you have associates who are guilty of such slips as—

> doan do that
> howja get there?
> wanna bet?
> ask 'em to go
> atta boy
> you gonna go, Pete?

When you hear any such slip, ask yourself, "Do I make any such mistakes?"

Follow this same plan when you listen to TV or radio. You'll find certain words that get clobbered almost every time they are used. You'll hear more at the office. Make a list of these words and when you use them try to give them their full and correct pronunciations.

You may say—

"Well, I'm pretty good at pronouncing the words I use." I am glad to hear that. But just check through these questions·

How do you pronounce the words—"get" and "forget?"

How do you indicate you mean—"yes?"

How do you pronounce the word ending—"ing?"

"How do you say the word—"you?"

Many of us say—

> "git" for "get"—"forgit" for "forget"
> "um" "unhuh" "yeah" and other sounds for "yes"
> "goin' " for "going"—"showin' " for "showing"
> "ya" and other sloppy sounds for "you"

Do you have any of these faults?

All such faults are due to carelessness, but since you have been guilty of them for a long time, it won't be too easy to correct them.

How to Correct These Faults

If you have any of these four faults, start trying to correct them. Here are some suggestions:

The "Git" Fault

All you need to do here is to say "get" for "git," "forget" for "forgit." It sounds easier than it will be, but work on it for a week and you'll find yourself starting to progress.

The "Yes" Fault

Say "yes" with more emphasis. You might try substituting another word, like "surely" or "certainly."

The "ing" Fault

I like the exercise of saying over and over—

going
knowing
showing
rowing

putting the emphasis on the "ing" syllable. The "ing" sounds beautiful; it rolls off the tongue. Try saying it fully—goING, showING, knowING, rowING.

The "You" Fault

To your listener "you' means him, and because of that it becomes a most important word to him. Start using the greeting, "How are YOU?" Show your interest by pronouncing the "you" carefully and fully.

Correct any one of these faults and listeners will notice the improvement in your speech almost immediately.

Practice With Your Name

When you have to say your name, do you say it so that others can understand it? When you introduce another, do you concentrate on saying his name so that it can be understood? You have been at meetings where those in attendance are asked to give their names, and as the strangers say their names you hear very few of them. This is because the speaker slurs over the sounds, speaks too fast, or not loud enough.

In my effort to remember names, I ask men who are introduced to me, "how do you spell your name?" They spell it, and I ask, "Is that pronounced so-and-so?" I have had men in my sessions say their names so sloppily that no one could understand what they said. I ask these men to stand and say their names again and perhaps again and again, until the others have a chance to understand the name. I ask them to slow down, to pronounce each syllable. I have learned to pronounce my name—Hegg-R-tee. Work out a device like this for your name. If you have a one-syllable name, slow up as you say it; if your name has more than one syllable, pronounce each syllable. Give the listener a chance to hear and understand what you said. Most of us would improve our speaking if we learned to say our name so that listeners could hear the correct pronunciation.

Try Reading Aloud

Demonstrate to yourself how much improvement you need in enunciation by selecting a paragraph from any printed piece and reading it aloud. You'll find that you go too fast to enunciate clearly. Start again, remembering the three bits of advice given in the last three chapters—

Slow up a bit,
Speak a bit louder, and
Try to pronounce each word clearly.

All three devices will help you move toward your TOP.

31

How to Develop a Voice That Makes People Want to Listen

How can a voice that annoys help an individual reach his TOP?

Every voice is different. You hear nine voices that are pleasant, then you hear one that somehow gets on your nerves.

Last week, an acquaintance was looking for a golf game at the club. One of my foursome said, "Tell him we are filled up." Since one of our foursome was uncertain, I said, "Maybe we aren't."

"Tell him we are anyway. His voice irritates me."

"But he is a good Joe."

"Maybe so, but that rasping voice will ruin my game."

So the irritating voice was out. Such a voice rules its owner out of many activities. Once my boss told me, "I know Chuck is the guy for this job, but I couldn't stand listening to that voice of his all day long."

You know voices you would rather not play with, work with, ride with. You'd prefer someone with a more pleasant voice.

When you hear a voice that bothers you, you wonder why the owner doesn't do something about it. It might pay to ask, "Does my voice annoy anybody?"

Three Ways Voices Bother Others

Your voice might bother others because of—

(a) its sound
(b) the attitude it displays
(c) the condition of your health it indicates.

Your Sound

Think of the words used to describe the unpleasant voice: shrill—strident—surly—growling—rasping—gravelly—grating—belligerent—loud—weak—whiny—go on, add to the list. If your voice can be described with any of those words, isn't it possible that associates judge you more by the sound of your voice than by what you say? I call an emcee on TV, "old whiny." I don't listen to his programs.

Your Attitude

Say, "How are you, Tom?" and Tom knows whether or not you care. Psychologists say that your voice can tell others that—

you are well-adjusted
you have the proper amount of self-esteem
you are confident
you are enthusiastic
you are willing to work
you want to be friends.

You know how you feel when the voice of the clerk in a retail store indicates that you are bothering him. He savs the words he should say but his attitude takes the feeling out of them.

The Condition of Your Health

I have mentioned that at times your voice tells the listener about your physical condition. A man in my speech clinic showed me a paragraph he had cut out of his company's employee magazine. It read—

"HOW NOT TO GET PROMOTED"

What chance of promotion do you think there is for an employee whose voice indicates that—

he hurts
he is tired
he is sleepy
he is not well.

What is such a person telling an executive who has the power to promote him?

You may know an associate whose tone of voice indicates that he is exhausted. He doesn't tell you in words, "I'm pooped out." His voice tells you. You wonder if his boss is pushing him too hard, but you don't feel that he should be moved into a tougher job.

How to Make Your Voice More Pleasant

William Norwood Brigance, in his book *Speech* (Appleton-Century-Crofts, Inc.), quotes a supervisior of announcers for NBC as saying, "Only five persons out of a hundred are born with good voices. The rest of us have to work for one." Professor Brigance qualifies that statement with the thought that the figure hinges on the definition of what a good voice is. Whether it is five out of a hundred or fifty out of a hundred, the figure shows that most of us can stand improvement. Here are some plans that have been tried by others with profitable results.

1. Consult a Voice Teacher

A teacher can suggest what to do about any voice faults that might bother others. He can work with you on getting more life into your voice and making it more pleasant to hear.

2. Study a Book on Voice Improvement

This will offer ideas you can use to make the most of your voice. It will give you exercises to help you improve your breathing, phonation, resonation, articulation.

3. Analyze Your Favorite Announcer

Select the one you feel has the most pleasing voice, and try to speak as he does. Don't try to imitate his voice. Stick with your voice, but try to figure out how he achieves the qualities you like. See if you can put the same feeling he does into what you say. Try for his timing.

4. Read Aloud to Your Wife

Read a paragraph from the newspaper aloud. Try to pronounce each word carefully. Ask your wife to listen, then read it a second time and ask if there has been any improvement. You'll do better the second time, I'm sure.

5. Read Children's Stories to Children

The youngsters will love any dramatics you put into the reading, and the dramatics will help the voice. Have Grandma in your story speak in the high voice, and the big bad wolf in a menacing voice. Let your voice indicate that he is the biggest, baddest wolf ever. If the story repeats a line over and over, after the first reading get the children to help you say that line. You say it distinctly and ask them to say it distinctly.

6. Recite Poetry

You have some verses that you liked when you studied them in high school, and after all these years the lines are still fresh in your memory—recite these lines now and then, with feeling: "The stag at eve had drunk his fill—," or "A few of the boys were whooping it up—."

Put energy into your voice; pronounce the words distinctly.

These lines by Oliver Wendell Holmes are to the point—

"Once more; speak clearly if you speak at all,
Carve every word before you let it fall—."

7. Join In Any Group Singing

Try to sing as loud as anybody. You say, "I can't sing." Neither can a lot of others, but they join in and get the voice exercise that helps them speak. I join in the songs at church and try to pronounce each word of the hymn. I sing out with gusto, perhaps bothering those around me, but I am practicing articulation. If your service club recites the pledge of allegiance before each meeting, say the words as if you mean them, a bit louder than you think necessary. Say each word clearly, show your enthusiasm for God, your country, the flag, and the republic. While you are doing this you will be improving your voice.

8. Use a Recorder

The tape recorder has become quite popular as a home entertainment device. You don't need one of the most expensive recorders to practice voice improvement. Recite a poem you know into it, and listen to the recording as you play it back. Don't dictate long pieces; one verse of a poem is enough. Dictate the same verse again, thinking of the mistakes the first playback revealed.

SELECT YOUR WORST FAULT

If it is a voice that sounds tired, put some energy into it. If it is weak, try to strengthen it. It is not difficult to correct any faults you have. In a short time you will see improvement, and listeners will think better of you because of any improvement. The pleasant voice makes friends—and friends help you move toward your TOP.

Does Your Voice Help You More?

All of the devices mentioned in the past four chapters are easy to try. I'm sure you have tried the ones you thought you needed, and have noticed improvement. Think back and check on what you have done:

1. What have been the results of your speaking a bit louder?
2. Did you need to speak a bit slower? When you spoke slower, did you seem to be easier to understand?
3. Then on enunciating more clearly—are you pronouncing that "ing" ending fully?
4. How have others responded to your efforts to cut the growl, the harshness, the shrill out of your voice?

If you have needed only a few of the improvements mentioned, and have taken care of even one of them, you have shown the spirit that takes an individual to his TOP.

32

Talking Your Way Towards Your Chosen "Top"

There is only one you. There is no duplicate anywhere.
Your ambition is to reach your own particular TOP.
Think positively about making it. You can if you desire to strongly enough.
Your "TOP" may be the position of the head of your department or company, the Grand PooBah of your lodge, or it may be some position that can make you of more service to your fellow men.
Whatever it is, organize your big mouth to help you make it. Anyone who converses with you judges you on what you say and how you say it. That's one way you appraise others, isn't it? Think of how you rate the one who—

has a weak voice
speaks with hesitation—"uns" and "ahs"
can't seem to explain clearly
tries to impress you with strange and fancy words
uses slurred expressions like—"gotta"—"cantcha"
makes usage mistakes like—"don't have no"
resorts to foul mouth.

You don't rate him high, do you? Make any of the mistakes listed or others mentioned in the preceding chapters, and your big mouth is tearing you down. There is no sense in allowing that to continue. The devices given to correct the fault are so easy to try and use. Use them and you will see improvement in a short time.

No other improvement can help you as much in your drive toward your TOP. Let your big mouth help you instead of hindering.

I wish you luck in your efforts to cut the confusion out of the great fog of yak-yak around us. Let listeners admire the clarity and common sense in what you say and how you say it.

May you reach your TOP, and God bless you and yours.

OTHER SELF-IMPROVEMENT BOOKS FROM <u>REWARD</u> THAT YOU WON'T WANT TO MISS!

☐ 08028-3 **Bottom Line Business Writing,** John S. Fielden and Ronald E. Dulek $6.95

☐ 10829-0 **Business Writing Style Book,** John S. Fielden and Jean D. Fielden $6.95

☐ 32154-7 **5,000 One and Two Liners for Any and Every Occasion,** Leopold Fechtner $4.95

☐ 35483-7 **Getting Through to People,** Jesse S. Nirenberg $5.95

☐ 37246-6 **Hand Analysis: A Technique for Knowledge of Self and Others,** Myrah Lawrance $4.95

☐ 38672-2 **Helping Yourself with E.S.P.,** Al G. Manning, D.D. $5.95

☐ 38662-3 **Helping Yourself with Self-Hypnosis,** Frank S. Caprio and Joseph R. Berger $5.95

☐ 40233-9 **How to Be Twice As Smart,** Scott Witt $6.95

☐ 41850-9 **How to Make One Million Dollars in Real Estate in Three Years Starting With No Cash,** Tyler Hicks $6.95

☐ 43528-9 **How to Talk Your Way to the Top,** Edward J. Hegarty $6.95

☐ 50366-4 **The Investment Evaluator,** Ronald Ady $9.95

☐ 54531-9 **Magic Power of Self-Image Psychology,** Maxwell Maltz $5.95

☐ 54889-1 **The Management of Time,** James T. McCay $4.95

☐ 68696-4 **Power with People,** James K. Van Fleet $4.95

☐ 79798-5 **Secrets of Mental Magic,** Vernon Howard $5.95

☐ 80347-8 **Self-Hypnotism,** Leslie M. LeCron $4.95

☐ 82390-6 **So You Want to Start a Business,** William Delaney $9.95

☐ 86043-7 **Successful Communication and Effective Speaking,** Millard Bennett and John D. Corrigan $4.95

☐ 90689-1 **Tested Advertising Methods,** John Caples $8.95

☐ 93495-0 **Twenty Steps to Power, Influence and Control Over People,** H.W. Gabriel $4.95

☐ 95202-8 **What Do You Mean I Can't Write,** John S. Fielden and Ronald E. Dulek $6.95

☐ 55069-9 **Managing Management Time,** William Oncken $19.95

Prices subject to change without notice.

BUY THEM AT YOUR LOCAL BOOKSTORE OR USE THIS HANDY COUPON

REWARD BOOKS — Dept. 4
Book Distribution Center
Route 59 at Brook Hill Drive
West Nyack, New York 10994

Please send me the books I have checked above. I am enclosing $_____ (please add 50¢ per copy to cover postage and handling). Send check or money order—no cash or C.O.D.'s. Please allow 4 weeks for delivery.

PLEASE

PRINT   Mr. Mrs.
             Ms. Miss

OR   Name...
             (circle one)

TYPE   Address...

             City................... State.... Zip..........

Dept. 4   BP 6831(2)